# HOW TO KILL
# ADVENTIST
# EDUCATION

*(and How to Give It a Fighting Chance!)*

## Shane Anderson

REVIEW AND HERALD® PUBLISHING ASSOCIATION

Since 1861 | www.reviewandherald.com

To order additional copies of *How to Kill Adventist Education,* by Shane Anderson, call **1-800-765-6955.**

Visit us at **www.reviewandherald.com** for information on other Review and Herald® products.

Copyright © 2009 by Review and Herald® Publishing Association

Published by Review and Herald® Publishing Association, Hagerstown, MD 21741-1119

Review and Herald® titles may be purchased in bulk for educational, business, fund-raising, or sales promotional use. For information, e-mail SpecialMarkets@reviewandherald.com.

The Review and Herald® Publishing Association publishes biblically based materials for spiritual, physical, and mental growth and Christian discipleship.

The author assumes full responsibility for the accuracy of all facts and quotations as cited in this book.

This book was
Edited by Gerald Wheeler
Copyedited by James Cavil
Cover design: Trent Truman
Cover image credits:
    Apple and books: © Stockxpert/JupiterImages
    Blackboard: © iStockphoto.com/dalton00
    Raised hands: © iStockphoto.com/urbancow
Interior design: Tina M. Ivany
Cover photo by 123RF
Typeset: Bembo 11/14

Unless otherwise indicated, texts are from the *Holy Bible, New International Version.* Copyright © 1973, 1978, 1984, International Bible Society. Used by permission of Zondervan Bible Publishers.

PRINTED IN U.S.A.

13  12  11  10  09                    5  4  3  2  1

**Library of Congress Cataloging-in-Publication Data**

Anderson, Shane, 1970-      .
How to kill Adventist education (and how to give it a fighting chance!) /Shane Anderson.
        p.cm.
1. Seventh-day Adventists—Education—United States.  I. Title.
LC586.A3A64 2009
370.1—dc22
                                        2008049333
ISBN 978-0-8280-2419-8

# DEDICATION

To my grandmother, Elva "Grackie" Pohl,
whose nearly nine decades of intellectual
pursuits continue to proclaim that Christians
should never stop learning.

# ACKNOWLEDGEMENTS

As with any sizable project, many people have provided invaluable assistance in the making of this book. My wife, Darlene, proved herself time and again to be a very patient and conscientious sounding board for my ideas, readily praising those that were good and graciously refining those that were half-baked. Dr. Gary Patterson, Dr. Dale Twomley, Dr. Donald Schafer (Senior), Don Schafer (Junior), Larry Marsh, Eileen States, and Rick Maloon all provided excellent feedback on manuscript drafts. Mark Thomas, Jeannette Johnson, Gerald Wheeler, and the entire editorial/publishing crew at the Review have been extraordinarily helpful in moving the book forward. And though not all of them are specifically cited in the pages ahead, I am indebted to the dozens and dozens of educators at all levels across the North American Division whose candid responses to my questions provided the foundation for the solutions *How to Kill Adventist Education* offers.

# CONTENTS

# PREFACE

I am very reluctant to write this book.

At first it seemed like a great idea: write down some ideas about Adventist education, throw in a vivid anecdote or two, and see what the Lord does with it. But after hammering away at this thing for quite some time, I am increasingly tempted to become nervous, tentative, and, yes, reluctant to publish what you'll find in the pages ahead.

Why? Because I am an *outsider*.

You see, I am not now, nor have I ever been a professional educator, much less one in the Adventist educational system.* I've never had to make lesson plans year after year; never taken a single course on how to be a professional teacher; and never had to learn to deal constantly with parents, students, and fellow teachers and staff with the intensity that professional teachers commonly experience throughout their careers. All of which has led me to ask an uncomfortable question: What fool would presume to write a book on the challenges facing Adventist education—much less how to actually *meet* those challenges—when they've never been a professional educator a day in their life?

Well, since you're now reading this book, I suppose that the fool . . . is me. But my prayer is that my foolishness will nonetheless prove helpful because of a single factor: perspective.

It is true that I'm not a professional teacher or school administrator. But in addition to having immense respect for those who are, I have been honored to be in close contact with a large number of education professionals for extended periods of time throughout my personal and professional life. As an Adventist pastor, all of the congregations that I've worked with have been constituents of Adventist schools. I've also served on a conference executive committee (which often dealt with the intimate and at times gritty details of primary and secondary school issues), and I've sat on the boards of multiple schools at both the primary and secondary levels. (And in case you're wondering, yes, I attended Adventist schools for all of my formal schooling from first grade through my master's degree.)

All of which brings me back to that point regarding perspective. Though

I am an "outsider," I have had significant contact with Adventist education in a variety of settings that has left me with some very distinct impressions as to what works in our schools and what doesn't. Like so many others before me, I too have wrestled with the reality of declining enrollment, declining funding, and declining enthusiasm for our educational system. I've fought long and hard for that system to become successful. And as time marches on and more and more schools close, I feel it would be irresponsible of me not to at least attempt to share some of my "foolishness" with others in the hope that my outsider's perspective might provide a unique vantage point that other schools can benefit from.

So consider yourself warned: much reluctant, outsider foolishness lies ahead! And may it be as much a blessing for you reading it as it has been for me writing it.

---

* As thrilling as it was, I'm reluctant to count my student missionary experience teaching high school one year in Micronesia as one of being "a professional educator."

# FOREWORD

Regardless of their church affiliations now, most former students of Adventist education have good feelings about it. My experience indicates that they will tell you that they were well prepared for their specific career pursuits and life in general. What they may have missed in academic rigor was more than compensated for by character development and work ethics. Nearly all of these products of Adventist education want to see their alma maters succeed and find it troubling and painful if and when their schools languish and/or close.

We all have examples of the gradual, steady decline in enrollment of Adventist schools. All of us have participated in many, shall we say, "ain't it awful" discussions (in closed and open forums) that seldom produced actionable ideas. And often when we came up with seemingly actionable ideas, the journey through the labyrinth of committees and church hierarchy was more than could be endured, even for this noblest of causes.

Shane Anderson has done all of us a great favor with his book. As my pastor, I have observed the same careful logic and arguments employed in his sermons now used in his book. With the precision of a prosecuting attorney he lays out virtually all of the problems (perceived and actual) in Adventist education today and then systematically provides step-by-step, spiritual, and actionable procedures to make measurable improvements. To God be the glory, there is empirical evidence that his recommendations really do produce measurable results.

In this book you will find something that *you* can do for the good of Adventist education. I too believe that quality Adventist education is an important component in improving the Adventist church and fulfilling the gospel commission. If you are motivated at all to advance Adventist education today, I believe you will find fresh and practical ideas here that will give Adventist education a fighting chance.

By the way, chapter 19 is worth the price of the book. Pastor Shane is at his best in this no-holds-barred discourse. If you get a little light-headed with "straight talk," you'd better stick with Dick and Jane.

— Dale Twomley

# INTRODUCTION:
## *The Incredible Vanishing School*

I'm a huge fan of Adventist education. Let me tell you why.

In my experience Adventist education is one of the most effective ways to prepare young people for the second coming of Christ. Furthermore, I believe that our schools—rightly run—are more successful at doing this than any other single evangelistic method, including Revelation seminars, church planting, felt-needs evangelism, or contemporary worship services. Also I believe that Adventist education has been the key to propagating our unique Adventist mission in the world. It has been the medium for sharing our values, finding our spouses, and raising Advent-minded families. Adventist education has even provided a nationwide and, yes, global sense of connectedness and community for more than 10 generations of students. And for the majority of our church's history, our schools have done highly significant work in guaranteeing that if Christ waits another generation before He returns, there will still be a faithful Adventist Church charging ahead, seeking to present souls to God for His kingdom. We are a called people, designed to be an end-time, Jesus-loving, Satan-crushing steamroller of a movement that passionately pursues Christ and His cause at the climax of history—and I believe that whatever our success has been at being that is, in very large part, a result of Adventist education.

All of which makes our current situation in the North American Division more than a little hard to swallow.

With a few encouraging exceptions, Adventist education in North America appears to be faltering. For instance, between 1980 and 2008 overall church membership in the North American Division (NAD) rose from 606,430 members to approximately[1] 1,082,900—a gain of 476,470 members, adding up to a 79 percent increase in that 28-year span of time.[2] Unfortunately, during that same period K-12 enrollment in the NAD decreased by 18,157 students. That equals a nearly 33 percent *drop* during the same period of time that the NAD *grew* by nearly 80 percent. (Indeed, it is part of a worldwide trend in Adventist education. As George Knight points out: "In 1945 the ratio of students in Adventist schools [worldwide] to church membership was 25 per 100. . . . But since [1965], the ratio has dropped off precipitously, to 15 per 100 in 1985 and 9 per 100 in 2000.") [3]

Sadly, this phenomenon of drastically declining school enrollment in spite of overall NAD growth takes on an additional dynamic when it comes to Adventist colleges and universities. According to a study published by the NAD and the Center for Creative Ministry, only an estimated 33 percent of eligible college-age Seventh-day Adventist students attend Adventist colleges and universities. *Fully two thirds of eligible Adventist college students choose non-Adventist schools.*

In light of such statistics, the resulting stories coming from our schools are predictably grim. Each successive school year brings word of yet another of our approximately 1,000 NAD school campuses either struggling mightily to survive or closing its doors altogether. Local school boards across the land meet late into the night, trying to figure out how to deal with still further declines in enrollment. Conference executive committees stare in despair as still another request for hundreds of thousands of dollars in "special subsidy" comes rolling in from their conference academy. And even some of our colleges, comparative giants though they may be, are having their share of severe financial and enrollment crises. (In fact, as I write this, one more of our longtime colleges is gearing up for a pivotal meeting that will seriously consider the destiny of the school—as in whether or not it will remain open.)

In the face of such problems, many of our school boards and staff members have taken heroic measures to right their respective ships. But honesty demands a painful admission: *More often than not, in spite of our best efforts, the decline has continued.* And the lack of progress has led many of us to give up, plop down in one of the deck chairs on our educational *Titanic,* and speak wistfully of the good old days when our schools (and perhaps even our coffers) were full. Too often we are a people both tired and grieved, waiting for the inevitable vortex of death to suck us down.

If that sounds overly dramatic, check things out for yourself. Take a hard look at the state of Adventist education in your own area and across our division. You will discover that in fact, we have a number of schools that are thriving[4]—perhaps even a few that have waiting lists of students clamoring to enroll. But those are in the minority. The majority of what you'll find consist of schools struggling not merely with shifting demographics or generational population dips, but also with severe, life-threatening problems, particularly among smaller elementary schools and boarding academies. (Another example: for the 2005-2006 school year the North Pacific Union Conference reported that it had 7,550 students enrolled in its K-12 program. Sounds good. But unfortunately, this represented a drop of *nearly 600 students compared with the previous five years.*)[5]

The resulting financial troubles that many conferences face are so severe that in some areas administrators are actively looking for ways to unload their conference-sponsored secondary education programs, hoping to turn them into local church constituent-run schools and in the process free up much-needed capital in the conference treasury for other projects.

Thus Adventist education finds itself at a crossroads. It is not the first time. But unless the church takes appropriate action soon, it may well be the last.

A brief word on this book's organization. We'll begin with a look at some of the commonly held misconceptions as to the root causes of Adventist educational decline. Then in part two we'll examine carefully what I believe are the true causes. In part three we'll consider what can kill struggling Adventist schools. Finally, in part four, we'll focus on possible solutions to the Adventist educational crisis.

So let's get to it! As you read, my hope is that in some small way this book will inspire you as an educational leader—which every one of you are if you have an interest in our children knowing Christ—to act boldly and implement the changes required for our schools to have a fighting chance at not merely surviving, but *thriving.* The "deceased" truly is not yet dead! And by the grace of God, we can yet turn the tide before it is too late.

---

[1] At this writing, NAD membership statistics for 2008 are not yet finalized. However, between 1997 and 2007, membership grew an average 1.95 percent each year. Using this average, we are able to extrapolate on the 2007 total and arrive at an approximate memebership for 2008.

[2] From a study done by Monte Sahlin published in the book *Trends, Attitudes, and Opinions: The Seventh-day Adventist Church in North America* (see p. 122 for a chart illustrating this trend). Available from AdventSource: 800-328-0525 or at www.adventsource.org.

[3] George R. Knight, in *Journal of Adventist Education,* Summer 2005.

[4] For instance, for the 2005-2006 school year, Walla Walla College (now Walla Walla University) had its highest enrollment in 20 years: 1,942 students. The late 1990s showed similar trents for Andrews University, Loma Linda University, Oakwood College, and Southwestern Adventist University.

[5] North Pacific Union Conference *Gleaner* (the official union paper), August 2006. Statistics taken from www.gleaneronline.org/101/8/29404.html.

# PART ONE

# THE SECONDARY CAUSES OF THE CURRENT CRISIS

# CHAPTER 1

# How We Didn't
# Quite Get Into This Mess

When fixing a problem, it's helpful to know not merely what it is, but what caused it. So let's look at a vital question: What brought Adventist education into the difficulties it currently faces?

When I have asked concerned Adventists this question, they give a fairly limited range of answers, such as the following:

"I don't know."

"Parents just aren't committed to Adventist institutions anymore."

"Adventist education is too expensive."

"We don't market our schools effectively enough. If more people knew about them, they would be thriving."

The trouble with such answers is twofold. First, they are usually followed by conversations that are lamentably short. A bit of speculation followed by a moving on to other subjects seems to satisfy our limited curiosity on the topic (or perhaps our fatalism sees further conversation as pointless). Second, while these answers all contain elements of helpful truth (with the possible exception of the first example), they don't grasp the true depth of the problem. Let's take a moment to analyze each of the last three answers briefly.

## The Death of Brand Loyalty

Take the idea of declining commitment to Adventist institutions. In days past, Adventists often took pride in their highly developed subculture (though we rarely put it in those terms). We had our own publications, our own traditions (popcorn and fruit at sundown on Sabbath), and of course, our own schools. In addition, we even had our own manufacturing facilities that produced choice morsels of food that no self-respecting Adventist potluck would be without. With only a little tongue in cheek, we could loudly proclaim that "our hope is built on nothing less than Worthington and Pacific Press."

But today there is little doubt that the heady days of Adventist brand loyalty are becoming a thing of the past. Many Adventists understand this intuitively already, but I'll share just one example of this trend in action to illustrate.

According to Harold Lee, former president of the Columbia Union Conference, a comparative study between Adventists and 28 other Protestant denominations reveals that "members are giving [money] far less today than in the past. In 1968 giving was at 10.8 percent of after-tax income. By 1996 it had declined to 4.5 percent. This decline represents a 58 percent decrease in the portion of income being given by church members. . . . Church members are voting with their feet and with their dollars."[1]

This leads to the obvious conclusion that Adventists are increasingly spending less and less to purchase Adventist "products"—educational or otherwise. How come?

Too often—particularly among older members—the response is simply that we aren't as loyal to Adventist institutions as we ought to be . . . *as though that were a complete answer in itself.* Far too often, members and education leaders that I have personally talked with in various portions of the United States have repeatedly retreated to this simplistic explanation, almost as though it were still 1955 and that institutional loyalty was still a widely held, finely tuned, and much-lauded part of the Adventist mind-set.

But it simply is not! Dedication to the "Adventist brand" is waning heavily . . . *and* the problems with Adventist education *go much deeper than a mere dearth of institutional loyalty.* In fact, flagging enthusiasm for SDA "brands" is *not* a core cause of Adventist educational decline, but rather another symptom of it (albeit an important one). Think of it this way: Do we really believe that there are large numbers of passionate, highly committed Seventh-day Adventists—*who also just happen to think that a school that would teach their children that that very same Adventism is not worth considering?* Of course not. Surely what we're seeing here is a lack of commitment not just to our schools or other institutions, *but to Adventism itself.* Here is the core of our current crisis (as we will discuss further shortly).

Please note that I'm not saying that if you send your kids to non-Adventist schools, you're not an Adventist. But I am most certainly declaring that we currently have large numbers of baptized Seventh-day Adventists—paid clergy and laity—who, while they think much of Christ and His grace, don't have much regard for Adventist claims to having a unique mission in the world. Furthermore, Adventism has spent much of the past two decades attempting to move itself into mainstream Western culture, and in so doing Adventism's reason for being has been, in my opinion, clouded—and thus, unavoidably, its educational system has been obscured as well. Again, more on this in chapter 2 and subsequent chapters.

## Too Costly?

What about the common thought that Adventist education is too expensive?

Certainly Adventist education is far from free (in some cases, *exceedingly* far). And, as we saw earlier, there exists a definite trend away from spending money on church-related institutions, one that certainly contributes both directly and indirectly to the perceptions of educational cost.

But the trouble with claiming high expense as a major reason for educational decline is that, depending on the school in question, such a claim can be answered *correctly* both "no, it's *not* too expensive" and "yes, it *is* too expensive." Here's how such a thing can be so:

Let's take the "no, it's not too expensive" crowd first. Proponents of Adventist education have often answered the charge of being overpriced with sound financial information to the contrary. They point out, for instance, that their particular Adventist school teaches Adventist values both by example and verbal instruction. For committed Adventists, this is of immense importance. Additionally, proponents note that if we also think in terms of above-average academics as well as extracurricular activities (cultural field trips, sports, advanced classes for qualified students, etc.) at their school, the "inexpensiveness" of Adventist education becomes even more apparent. They further point out that there is precious little financial profit—if any—built into the tuition and fees of Adventist schools—parents are paying for what they're getting, and often at a price that approaches bargain status.

This can be doubly true when one compares certain facets of Adventist schools to their public school counterparts. Many of our teachers, for instance—particularly long-tenured or postsecondary teachers—receive markedly lower wages in comparison to their peers in the public school system. (Translation: Those high tuition bills aren't there to make our teachers rich!) Or consider this: In some of the areas in which I've been associated with our schools, the expense required to educate one student in an Adventist school has been significantly lower than that required in the area public schools. Of course, Adventist parents, even though they may send their kids to Adventist schools, still have to pay local and state taxes. But the cost comparison between the two systems is nonetheless helpful in shedding light on the relative affordability of many of our schools.

All this adds up to the conclusion that when compared to other types of schools, Adventist institutions are often reasonably priced for what's being offered. (I remember the story of one of our most expensive academies being visited by some non-Adventist parents to see if their child might attend there. When they heard the price of tuition, they immediately and in complete seriousness asked, "What's wrong with your school?" They couldn't imagine how a quality Christian education could be so comparatively inexpensive.)

So based on what their school offers, these proponents argue that while Adventist education is not what we would call cheap, their particular school is reasonably priced when viewed within an Adventist values, academic, and extracurricular activity perspective.

Are they correct?

Probably so—again, for their particular school. And at the very least, such testimony ought to be good incentive for parents to take a second look at the perceived "over-priced-ness" of their school's tuition. It may be that upon inspection of the alternatives, they will find that Adventist school to be a relative bargain instead of a bank-busting lemon of an education.

But what about the "yes, it is too expensive" crowd? Can they too be correct in their assessment of Adventist education? They can, and in at least four ways.

First, for those church members not overly concerned about propagating Adventist values to their children, Adventist education does indeed appear overly expensive. It simply offers a product they are not interested in, and they will instead choose a good Christian school (usually closer to home geographically) or a quality public school.

Second, there are what we might call the "moderately committed" Adventists who want to send their children to Adventist school, but only if it's conveniently priced. They truly like their church and want their children to grow to share that affection through Adventist education, but only as long as it's relatively easy to do so within their perceived budgetary constraints.

I say "*perceived* budgetary constraints" because while this particular type of Adventist truly likes their church, they are often also fond of their Jet Skis, SUVs, and big-screen TVs. And when push comes to shove, the toys win out over tuition. Thus, for them, school tuition is indeed too expensive.

(Allow me a brief sermon here. I am not saying it is of necessity a sin to have the toys. Abraham, as I recall, was lavishly wealthy and had the hardware to prove it. But I am saying that hedonism and selfishness may be coming to play far too great a role among some Adventists when it comes to making educational choices for their kids. And if Adventists profess affection for their church and then send their children to non-Adventist schools because it's "just too expensive" to do otherwise—all the while pouring large chunks of money into fun toys that will nonetheless burn when Jesus returns—then perhaps it's time for a little honesty. Big tuition bills may not be the problem. Instead it may be misplaced priorities, which leads to the obvious question: Which is more important in the scope of eternity? The toys/cars/house/etc.? Or potentially eternal life for one's kids? True, Adventist education can't guarantee that one's children will be in heaven. But in the spirituality department, it'll blow our jet skis into the weeds nearly every time.)

Third, even for Adventists who *are* heavily committed to their God and their church, there is absolutely no doubt that while Adventist education may be a relative bargain for what you get in return, it can still cost a ton of money! Ten to eighteen thousand dollars for a year at our boarding academies, for instance, is the norm. *And that's for a high school, not a college education!* For lower- and middle-income families, that price tag can be a real challenge to meet. (And speaking of high school/college tuition parity, a parent recently remarked to me what a relief it would be to have their student go to James Madison University, a nationally respected school in central Virginia. The reason for that relief? The yearly tuition would be a mere $6,000 per year—about $11,000 less than that charged for a boarding student at the Adventist academy their daughter was graduating from!)

Keen observers will note that some non-Adventist schools (such as the aforementioned James Madison University) have some financial resources—big endowments, eligibility for certain grants—that we don't have and thus we can't be expected to offer their (in some instances) lower prices. Granted. But ultimately that may be beside the point. The bottom line still is that Adventist education, even for the dedicated lower-to-middle income member, is becoming very highly priced indeed. And if the trend of increasing tuition continues, and we do not come up with commensurate financial aid resources, we may not only price ourselves out of the market, we may also eliminate all but the very well-heeled.

Fourth and last, for those parents who are deeply concerned about passing on Adventist values, Adventist education too often is also deemed too expensive for them . . . *because the particular school they're looking at isn't particularly Adventist.* Whether it's a fuzzy focus on Christ or a lack of emphasis on the unique mission, values, and standards of Adventism, in my experience many of our schools lack a sufficiently Adventist flavor, and Adventist parents increasingly aren't willing to pay the price to send their kids to such institutions.

And no wonder such parents are concerned! At the risk of stating the obvious, Adventist education should seek to achieve a goal far greater than superior academics, outstanding extracurricular activities, or even superior character development, as important as all these may be. It should seek to *establish in our children a personal relationship with Jesus Christ so that they may be lifelong Seventh-day Adventist witnesses for Him.* And if that unique goal is absent, devout Adventist parents rightly look at high tuition prices and deem correctly that they are indeed too expensive! *The "Adventist flavor" issue is vital,* and we will discuss it more shortly.

Obviously the question of the price of tuition is a major concern when discerning the causes of Adventist educational decline. We'll explore ways to deal with this in chapter 18.

## Are We Poorly Marketed?

What about the idea that inferior marketing accounts for a large share of our schools' demise?

I mean no harm when I say that in my experience, many of our schools (and churches, for that matter), while not intentionally so, are not experts in presenting themselves to their communities. Most school leaders understandably are not marketing professionals and may lack the money, time, and other resources to become marketing-savvy.

But that said, let's be certain that we understand *whom* we feel that we are missing through a lack of marketing skill. Almost always, when I've heard Adventists calling for better promotion of our schools, the goal is to try to reach *non*-Adventists—an intriguing focus given our recent "marketing history."

Most people would agree that the promotional programs of many of our schools today, challenged though they are, are in many ways an improvement when compared to those of the schools of the 1970s and 1980s. In those days mass mailings, community focus groups, demographic studies, niche marketing techniques, etc., were not high on most of our schools to-do lists. But here's the irony: While Adventist education is struggling today, on the whole it was *thriving* 20 and 30 years ago—a time when our marketing efforts were supposedly inferior. Why did we thrive back then, even with subpar marketing approaches?

It is not because of some mysterious magnetism that we had in the 1970s and 1980s (though I've always thought that those big-hair and polyester pants pictures on our brochures from that era did have a certain magnetism about them . . . ), but rather something much more mundane that we discussed earlier in this chapter: *Adventists of that time naturally filled our schools.* It's just what we as Adventists did (though most did *not* do so mindlessly—they had a reason for their choice, as we'll explore later). Adventist parents had Adventist kids who enrolled in Adventist schools.

But today they don't—certainly not in the numbers they did in the past. And since most schools often aren't sure *why* they don't, they can't pursue those Adventists with the proper enticements. So we have instead turned to marketing to *non*-Adventists. "If we can just get the word out about the great things going on at our school, non-Adventist parents will be much more likely to send their kids to our school," we say. And certainly some non-Adventist students would come to our schools if they were properly marketed to.

But not many.

I wish I could say otherwise, but experience is a good teacher, and with very few exceptions,[2] my observation has been that even the best of marketing to non-Adventists rarely yields the results that we crave. The scenario I've encountered usually runs something like this. An Adventist school gets another drop in enrollment. The board convenes and determines that marketing to the community is the answer. After much thought and many late nights, they have a stack of shiny, high-quality brochures printed up. They form a plan of attack, with the principal and/or board members setting up meetings with various community leaders, students doing door-to-door work, etc.—all in an effort to get the word out about the legitimately great things going on at that Adventist school. And then . . . few—if any—from the community sign up the next school year. The principal is frustrated, the school is out a chunk of change, and the enrollment continues its downward slide.

And why don't those community families register their kids after seeing our shiny brochures and hearing our heartfelt spiels? There are a number of reasons, but right near the top is *that we Adventists are unique—and, in the eyes of many non-Adventists, downright strange.* For instance, we go to church on the "wrong" day; we belong to a comparatively small but growing "cult"; and we seem to enjoy substantial amounts of vegetarian food (though I have learned that this last point was not nearly so weird in Seattle as it is in my current home in rural Virginia). And non-Adventist, Sundaygoing (and non-Sundaygoing), mainstream, carnivorous parents generally sense this strangeness and are accordingly cautious. They understand that schools tend to teach values that last a lifetime. And so they rightly ask: "Do we want our children to become Adventists?" A reasonable chance of that happening exists if their kids go to an Adventist school. So these parents are careful and, in my experience, rarely choose to come to our schools in any significant numbers. Our schools in this sense (and, I should add, in the North American Division) are not generally the community-targeting evangelistic powerhouses that some have imagined them to be.

(I must point out that this is not to say that I agree with the tired old saw that declares, "Adventist *churches* are small and should be because we have a unique message." I do not believe this, and as far as local *congregations* are concerned, we need to learn that our uniqueness is our best calling card when it comes to public and personal evangelism. But I hasten to add that there is a vastly different dynamic that occurs in a local *church* as compared to that which occurs in a local church *school*. At the church the parents are usually the guests who are checking Adventism out, then—

if the parents give the all-clear—the children may possibly follow. But at the local school, while the parent may do some initial scouting out of things, it's the child who's day in, day out being exposed to a new and potentially contagious religion—and that reality is simply more than most non-Adventist parents are willing to experiment with. Church? Often, yes. School? Usually no.)

So what to do?

In my opinion, marketing to non-Adventists should be done, but only as extra time and money allow. Instead, we should spend the bulk of our time promoting to (drum roll, please) *Adventists*. After all, there are tens of thousands of Adventist student-aged kids—the ones who would most naturally come to our schools—who already know that our schools exist *and still do not attend.*

They do not attend for a variety of reasons, and in a bit we'll talk about some possible ways to overcome those. But I'll spill the beans some now and say that most of the time *Adventist education and in particular its benefits are grossly undercommunicated to our members.* Putting an ad in the union paper can be affirming for the already-convinced,[3] but it just doesn't cut it for most "nonenrolling" Adventists when it comes to being convinced of the necessity of Adventist education. Much more is required, and until the venues, content, and volume of "parent education"—aka marketing—are improved, we will continue to see Adventist parents choosing to send their students elsewhere.

*So?*

Now that we've looked at some secondary causes of the problem of Adventist educational decline—waning commitment to Adventist institutions, tuition costs, and poor marketing—let's get to the primary causes. I believe the six primary factors behind Adventist educational decline are:

1. The lack of passion among churchgoing members for being a "conservative" Seventh-day Adventist.
2. A misunderstanding of what constitutes biblical discipleship.
3. Poor pastoral support of Adventist education.
4. Poor parenting.
5. The inroads of postmodernism, secularism, and "liberalism" in Adventism.
6. Poor-quality schools.

Knowing *almost* how we got into this mess will not suffice. Instead we've got to uncover these deeper, more core reasons that Adventist education is in decline. Only then can we understand what steps to take to move our schools back into health. Part two will look at each one of the above causes in detail.

---

[1] Harold L. Lee, "Church Structure in 2025," www.adventistreview.org/thisweek/millenn5.htm.

[2] There will probably always be outstanding examples of schools that have a high percentage of non-Adventist students (such as our school on Orcas Island in the state of Washington, Olney Prep School in Maryland, etc.). But in the North American Division they are in the minority. (Outside of the NAD? That's a different story.)

[3] Kudos to Andrews University, Southwestern Adventist University, and Southern University for already sending marketing material to my two daughters, who are currently 2 and 7 years old.

PART TWO:

# THE ROOT CAUSES
# OF THE CURRENT CRISIS

# CHAPTER 2

# It's Hard to Be Excited
# About What You Don't Value

## "We Are Asleep"

One of the top reasons for Adventist educational decline is *the lack of passion among churchgoing members for being a "conservative" Seventh-day Adventist.* That statement is sure to raise some eyebrows for at least two reasons.

First, thoughtful readers may want to classify this as a secondary rather than primary cause of educational decline, since such a lack of passion may result from wider cultural trends (for instance, the postmodern thought and secularism that are part and parcel of the challenges facing our schools). To those of you who take this view, your point is well taken, and chapter 6 (which will deal with this very issue in more detail) should be seen as a hand-in-glove partner with this chapter.

Second, the notion that a lack of passion today for being a "conservative" Seventh-day Adventist as a main cause of educational decline can be problematic simply because the term *conservative* seems pejorative to many Adventists and hardly desirable as a label for oneself. The word has become linked with such inspiring connotations as "legalistic," "prudish," "unhappy," "cheese-free," and—most damning of all in our day and age—"boring." Add to this that the precise definition of a "conservative" Adventist can be a bit of a moving target (thus the quotation marks), and any discussion about "conservative" Adventism appears to be ill-advised at best.

But let's live dangerously for a moment and begin to tackle that discussion anyway. I'll talk in depth about how I define such a "conservative" Adventist later on. But I will drop a few hints now by pointing out that I believe there ought to be a great deal of room today in our church for discussion and disagreement. We do not all need to be the same. Cookie-cutter Adventists are generally boring to others and (in their more honest moments) to themselves. (Some of the worst sermons Adventists preachers preach today are the ones that everyone present agrees with and that cause absolutely no hint of dissension—sermons far from the great tradition of riotous preaching by Jesus, Paul, and others [for example, Luke 4:14-30; John 10:22-39; Acts 19:23-31].) So I'm not suggesting that we aim to be "conservative" Adventists in a facsimile, carbon-copy sort of way.

*But I am saying that we Adventists—even those who attend church regularly— have generally lost our common core.* Being "conservative" in the sense of passionately striving to preserve, steward, and propagate our unique Adventist mission and calling in the world has gone largely by the wayside. To be blunt, we are "in the church," attend services, and may even pay tithe, *but we too often don't know who we are as Adventists anymore.* And at times we don't care.

Does Adventism really have a unique role to play in the world? We're not sure. Does Adventism need to be so distinct as to have its own publications, schools, etc.? Again, we can't say. Furthermore, we don't read Ellen White much anymore, and—far more ominously—surveys have repeatedly told us that the majority of us don't read the Bible, either, at least not in any serious way that, coupled with prayer, brings revival and revolution to our dusty souls.

Even "the landmarks" of our Adventist faith—the beliefs regarding the Sabbath, the state of the dead, the sanctuary, the nearness of Christ's coming—have become increasingly vague and irrelevant to large swaths of our North American Division membership. It's not that we are particularly hostile to these unique beliefs (though certainly emotional discussions do arise occasionally regarding them). Rather, we have too often simply stopped caring about them, stopped discussing them, stopped studying them. "We are," as one of my former theology professors recently put it, "asleep."

## How Did This Happen?

Undoubtedly, the causes of our spiritual sedation run decades deep and could take quite a bit of ink to unravel (and again, chapter 6 will explore this more deeply). But in the interest of brevity, let's draw some quick and hopefully useful conclusions.

One of the primary reasons for our current lack of passion for Adventism is undoubtedly our backlash against the legalism (both real and imagined) of the 1940s, 1950s, and 1960s. Youth who felt they were being beaten over the head with the Sabbath or Ellen White, for instance, grew older, got out of the house, and yes, often tended to avoid both Sabbath seriousness and Ellen White's writings.

I remember hearing a teacher in one of our colleges state very clearly (and with not a little emotion) that he and his fellow classmates had been abused by their academy teachers. Consequently, this teacher (and others) then resolved to spare their own students a similar fate if they ever taught in Adventist schools. Their plan for implementing such "safe" instruction? Don't talk about the unique aspects of Adventism. No, don't bad-mouth or malign the church, but don't dwell on its unique mission, either. And by this professor's own admission, that is precisely what he and a host of colleagues have done around the division.

Interestingly, the ValueGenesis study perhaps unintentionally added fuel to this "code of silence" when it revealed our youths' lack of grace orientation. It sent pastors and teachers across the NAD scrambling to discover and/or help others discover the grace of Jesus Christ. Praise the Lord! However, the renewed and much-needed emphasis on grace seemed to give (for some Adventists, at least) even more credence to suppress Adventist uniqueness—a uniqueness that many viewed as being in opposition to grace.

The results of this type of classroom instruction—which neither maligns nor widely speaks of Adventism—are both varied and very much with us today. The good news is that today, in part thanks to such teachers and pastors, legalism in the Seventh-day Adventist Church is truly hard to come by (a few rural holdouts notwithstanding). Again, praise the Lord! But on the down side, *we have too often replaced legalism with ignorance of, apathy toward, and waywardness from the unique primary mission of the Seventh-day Adventist Church.*

Perhaps we should have expected such a shift. When we are wounded by something spiritually, we tend to swing hard the other direction when righting whatever was wrong. As we discover the grace of God for the first time or afresh, we often put a lot of distance between us and any perceived vestiges of legalism. Additionally, other non-Adventist churches that have focused for years on the grace of Christ can become attractive, which can have some benefits as we learn from their perspectives. We crave grace and the fellowship of others who feel the same.

## The Need for Both Sides of the Coin

But if we are not wise, this trend can lead (and I believe has done so) to something as equally damaging as legalism, and that is libertinism—doing our own thing because (as the ancient saying goes) we are "under grace, not law."

Such sentiments would have been unimaginable 50 years ago, but today they are commonplace in the Adventist Church. For instance, I've heard some of my pastor friends reflect shades of this thinking when they point out that "_____ [insert the name of any prominent Sundaygoing church] doesn't keep Sabbath, yet look how much the Lord has blessed them!" The obvious conclusion is that if such omissions are good enough for them, it ought to be good enough for us.

The liberating truth (and part of the increasingly unique message that Adventism is to carry to the world) is that grace and law are but two sides of the same coin. To have law without grace is to be doomed to despair and disappointment. But to have grace without law is to be lost—that is, directionless, to know not where one is going or in which direction God lies. We are saved that we might serve (Eph. 2:10), and that service will inevitably be carried out according to the laws that God has set for our joy and development. When one has been saved by grace, free and full, God's law becomes candy for the soul, a sacred gift that helps explain how life works best. No wonder David repeatedly dedicated entire psalms to the praise of God's law! And only those who grow to reverence fully and passionately pursue both the grace and the law of God are able to find true fulfillment—that is, Jesus Christ—in this life and the next.

But with that mature balance lacking, any Adventist trying to apprehend afresh the power and passion of the Advent movement as God intends it to be is sure to falter. Claims of "uniqueness" will continue to lose out to poorly constructed but popular views of "grace." Unless we intentionally intervene in the North American church to solve this problem—that is, unless we can so educate our members that they embrace anew and with vigor the unique primary mission of the Adventist Church—we will continue to see a steady stream of Adventists who lack a passion for what God calls them to be. The church will continue to fade in this division, and our work will grind ever more slowly.

And lest we forget, the lethal assault already in progress on Adventist education will also continue. *For when we are murky on or uninterested in the uniqueness of Adventism, we are far less inclined to send our kids to Adventist schools.*

(And note carefully: I respectfully submit that this murkiness takes on an added twist when the one who is murky is also a teacher or administrator in an Adventist school. I'll address this in more detail later in chapter 7. But for now, suffice it to say that if a situation were to exist in which we have, on the one hand, parents who don't grasp the unique mission of Adventism, and, on the other hand, school staff who also don't understand it, the prospects for our students graduating as passionate, Spirit-filled, in-it-for-the-long-haul Adventists seriously diminish.)

*This is a genuine crisis in our division—perhaps the greatest one that we currently face.* While certainly passionate, "conservative" Adventists do still dwell in our midst, they are increasingly a rare (and often silent) breed. And if this trend continues, NAD Adventism's identity crisis will continue to grow. As Reinder Bruinsma rightly points out: "The greatest challenge of the church's educational institutions around the world is to maintain a clear Adventist identity in what is being taught and in everyday life on campus."[*] We have got to rediscover who we are and why we are here, or else our schools will continue to falter.

---

[*] Reinder Bruinsma, "The Quest for Integrity: Facing the Key Challenge of Postmodernism," *Journal of Adventist Education* 69, no. 1 (October/November 2006): 18.

# CHAPTER 3

# The Importance of
# Barking Up the Right Tree

Let it be trumpeted loud and clear: Many of the root causes of the demise of Adventist schools do not lie in the institutions themselves. They reside instead in the local church. And those factors have a great deal to do with the practice of what we commonly call "discipleship."

Now, this is not a book on the intricacies of making disciples for Christ. We have other resources available for that purpose.[1] But I will briefly summarize some of the elements of discipleship, as they are pivotal to understanding the crisis in Adventist education. Hang with me here, for though it may appear that we're momentarily going far afield, I think that you will see clearly in the end that we are most definitely not.

## The Unique Adventist Mission

If you asked 10 average Adventists what the unique primary[2] mission of the Adventist church is, what do you think they'd say? My experience is: at least 11 different things! When I've asked audiences across the United States this question, the answers to begin with are usually quite general: "To serve God," "To worship God," "To serve others," "To make disciples," etc. But then I point out that surely other Christian churches have this as their primary mission too. "What's the primary uniquely *Adventist* mission?" I then persist. And what often follows is . . . prolonged silence (and it doesn't seem to matter if the group consists of laity, clergy, or administrators). And in the interest of full disclosure, for too long a time I would have responded with such silence myself!

But ignorance is a good motivator, and after a lot of prayer, study, and pain, I think today I've got a reasonable handle on what our unique primary mission is. It goes like this (and let me quickly say that what follows is definitely the *Reader's Digest* version—one could write reams on the topic).

My favorite way of summarizing our uniquely Adventist primary mission is to say that it is:

# "To make fully devoted followers of Christ who help others biblically withstand the final deception."

Let's unpack that. First, careful readers will note that the statement combines the Great Commission of Matthew 28:18-20 and the three angels' messages in Revelation 14:6-12.

Let's reverse the order and start with the three angels. Entire books could (and should) be written on their messages. But a few observations will suffice for our discussion now.

Adventists have always had a special stake in Revelation 14:6-12, for the three angels are at the core of what gives us our primary and uniquely Adventist mission. In the three angels we see that God has called us not only to make disciples, but to do so in the specific context of a world fast approaching its end (verse 7: "the hour of his [final] judgment has come") and a world characterized by deception much more than it is by truth (see verse 8 regarding Babylon and verse 9 concerning the mark of the beast, etc.). The Lord summons Adventism to reveal the true nature of Babylon's[3] deceptions about Christ, so that people may see clearly His love and His way of life. (This is indeed the core purpose of preaching such doctrines as the state of the dead, the Sabbath, the sanctuary, etc.—to clear away this multifaceted "final deception" package so that humanity might find Christ.)

I cannot emphasize it enough: *This apocalyptic mind-set is one of the most defining and important characteristics that Adventism possesses.* We believe that Jesus is coming sooner, not later. That's one reason we refer to ourselves as "Adventists"! And consequently, all that we do we must carry out in that mind-set—not as a people that are frantic or scared because the end of time is imminent, but rather as a people craving the appearing of their Friend, Lord, and Master, Jesus Christ. This is the heart and soul of the three angels' messages.

Moving on quickly now, what about the first part of our unique primary mission involving the Great Commission? In Matthew 28 Jesus, in the most authoritative statement He ever made while on earth (see verse 18), commands every Christian to be about the work of making disciples of Christ, disciples whom Jesus describes as being taught "everything I have commanded you" (verse 20). They are mature disciples, knowing and seeking to live out the whole of what the Bible commands them to do and be (see also Eph. 4:13-15). And note carefully: *If a church of whatever stripe—Baptist, Methodist, Catholic, or Adventist—is not about the business of making such genuine, mature disciples of Christ, then regardless of the name on the church sign, it is not a Christian church.*

Furthermore, the magnitude of this calling to make disciples only intensifies when we realize that creating genuine, mature followers of Christ is neither easy nor accidental. It is instead an *intentional* process whereby we *mentor* new believers into becoming disciple multipliers, in which pagan "Joe Six-Pack" literally becomes church member "Joe Missionary," sooner or later helping to bring others into the kingdom. (When we look around our pews and see how few "Joe Missionaries" there are, we begin to realize how difficult it has become to disciple our members.)

Still with me? We'll circle back to Adventist education soon, so let's keep going.

## From Beer to Missions

Part of this beer-to-missions transformation for "Joe" occurs in ways that we're pretty adept at as a church, such as through the conveying of discipleship information in a Sabbath school class. But the greater part of discipleship—the mentoring part—can occur only in one-to-one or small group settings in which more-experienced believers *model* specific disciplines, practices, and habits for less-experienced ones. This process of discipleship obviously lasts a lifetime, but the basics of it take three or four years of intentional interaction between "student" and "teacher" (much akin to what Jesus did in His three and a half years on earth).

At the conclusion of that three- or four-year span of time, the *mentored* and *modeled-for* disciple needs to also be "*mantled*"—that is, publicly given the mantle of service, indicating to the assembled church that the disciple has achieved a measure of maturity in Christ and is now ready to pursue the discipling of others both within and outside of the community of faith with full vigor and passion. This mantling process is chronologically short, but long on significance, and often makes or breaks a disciple's effectiveness in ministry. (In case you're wondering, Jesus mantled His disciples on at least two occasions—first in Matthew 10 and a second time at Pentecost in Acts 2.)

So we now come to one of several foundational discipleship truths: *The process of mentoring/modeling and mantling is part and parcel of fulfilling Jesus' call to make disciples.* And without this discipleship process, most Adventists become stunted in their growth and either leave the church (a lack of intentional discipleship is one of the top causes of the swinging back door in our churches) or stick around and become mere pew warmers—and it is difficult to say which outcome is more damaging to the cause of Christ.

We're almost there. Keep reading!

## A Dual Passion

So what does this mean with regard to our primary mission "to make fully devoted followers of Christ who help others biblically withstand the final deception"? Just this:

I believe Adventist churches today generally err on one of two sides when it comes to fulfilling our unique primary mission. We either rarely or never carry out the three angels' portion of our mission and reveal Babylon's deceptions (in which case we might as well sell our assets and join another Sabbathkeeping denomination); or we focus on the apocalyptic portion of our calling at the expense of our calling to make disciples—*almost as though our prophetic message exempted us from developing people into genuine, mature disciples.* (I hasten to add that Adventism is hardly alone in its lack of discipleship. Nearly every other denomination under the sun faces great challenges in this area. A lack of genuine Christian disciple making will surely be one of the primary factors in the establishment of such things as the mark of the beast—an institution with a veneer of Christianity, but devoid of its reality, devoid of genuine discipleship.)

The truth is, of course, *that Adventists ought to be passionate about doing* both *things!* We ought ardently to proclaim the three angels, removing the deceptive scales from peoples' eyes *and* simultaneously making genuine, mature disciples of Christ. We are called to know Christ and to make Him known, to prepare the world for His second coming through obedience to the Great Commission *and* the proclamation of the three angels. That is our primary calling, and anything less represents a suicidal departure from our reason for being.

## Hey, We Made It!

And now, at last, we can ask: What does all this talk about Adventist mission and discipleship have to do with the demise of Adventist education?

Just this: *a direct correlation exists between the emphasis placed on Adventist discipleship in the local church and the level of support shown for the discipleship that is Adventist education.*

Let's face it: The local church—not the school—gets first crack at most young Adventists and their parents. And the local church—not the school—has the first opportunity to educate believers new and old as to what is expected of them in Christ. And when the local church, either by word or deed, says, "Baptism, mental assent to a few key doctrines, and church service attendance are enough; you will be a member in good and regular standing if you do these things," it's no wonder that parents are unwilling to fork over thousands of dollars for some Adventist schoolteacher to perform an apparently unnecessary function in the discipling of their kids!

Moreover, when a local Adventist congregation has no tangible discipleship process and thus gives no concrete indication that baptism is only a beginning and not the end, the entire spiritual growth process is cheapened, including the preparation required for baptism. Certainly Adventist parents want their children to be baptized. But again, if all that baptism in the Adventist Church means is that now you believe a few unique things, spectate at church each week, and eat Special K loaf at potluck, the urgency for parents to actually pay someone to help them achieve that end becomes seriously diminished.

And tragically, the problem goes still deeper. For when the nature of genuine *Adventist* discipleship—that is, discipleship that passionately conveys the primary and unique Adventist mission, as well as Adventist values and concepts—is misunderstood, it allows other forms of discipleship to naturally take over.

You see, the bad news is that discipleship—Adventist or otherwise—occurs with our children *whether we wish it to or not.* Every day the people that our children come into contact with are mentoring them. It may be for evil or for good, but the fact that mentoring will take place is irrefutable. Those whom our children admire will shape their destiny. If we intentionally allow a non-Christian authority—such as a non-Christian public high school teacher—in a discipling role in our kids' lives, our kids will quickly learn that Christ is optional in making life decisions. And even if that public high school teacher is a Christian but (for instance) does not keep the Sabbath, we practically shout to our children that the Sabbath is nothing more than a personal preference. The cost of improper discipleship of our children is thus potentially eternal.

(Please note that this is not to say that we can't learn from non-Adventists. If that were the case, Adventism would be doomed very quickly to intellectual inbreeding and subsequent stagnation—and I hate it when that happens. But learning from non-Adventists for *younger* children is a very, very risky proposition because of what I hope are obvious reasons. I remember one family who came up to me at a camp meeting once after I gave the Sabbath morning sermon on how important it was for us to mingle with non-SDAs and non-Christians. They were very excited, and immediately asked if I thought it was a good idea to transfer their kids to a public high school to be "salt and light" there. It visibly took them aback when I suggested that, unless their children were exceedingly mature in their faith for their age, it would almost certainly be a bad idea. But that's reality. Our children, in their formative years,[4] need Adventist role models—mentors—who live out what it means to be a joyful, faithful Seventh-day Adventist disciple of Christ.)

Of course, the wonderful truth about Adventist education is that when done correctly, *it is genuine Christian/Adventist discipleship.* It is the training of our children of whatever age to follow Christ, to relate to Him, to know His creation, to be His agents of life in all areas of society (more on this later)—and yes, to be faithful Seventh-day Adventists who prepare others to stand in the final crisis before Christ returns. And when parents recognize the enormity of this discipleship task—when they realize that to be a Seventh-day Adventist disciple of Jesus, their children will need other mature Seventh-day Adventists to *mentor* them in Christ, to daily *model* for them the Christian faith, and to begin to *mantle* them for service—then those parents will willingly shoulder any reasonable cost to see godly Seventh-day Adventist teachers disciple their children for seven or eight hours a day, five days a week.

*But lacking such an understanding of Seventh-day Adventist mission and disci-*

*pleship and the level of mentoring those things require, support for Adventist educa-*
*tion dwindles dramatically*—and the blame lies first at the door of the local
church, not the school.

"But," you might say, "what about the schools that don't take that call to
make genuine *Seventh-day Adventist* Christian disciples seriously?" Great question, and we'll get there. But let's continue with some other concerns first.

---

[1] Philip Samaan's *Christ's Way of Making Disciples* (Hagerstown, Md.: Review and Herald,
1999) is an excellent book on this topic.

[2] Every church has more than one mission. I am not suggesting here that what follows
constitutes Adventism's one and only mission in the world, but rather that it constitutes its primary (in the first place, of greatest importance) mission.

[3] Often we have too narrowly defined Babylon's identity. I believe that any group of people or organization that teaches others (1) that we must work our way into God's love or (2)
that we must replace God's law with something of our own creation is Babylon—be they
Catholic, Protestant, pagan, or Seventh-day Adventist.

[4] "Formative years" obviously implies different things for different people. From a discipleship perspective, I believe that it means that our children should attend Adventist schools
at least through high school. And from a marriage perspective, attendance through college
seems entirely logical.

# CHAPTER 4

# The Pastor and the Incredible Shrinking School

In spite of the downgrading in the general public eye of the value of ministers, Adventist pastors still carry tremendous influence in our denomination. Our brothers and sisters in the division office may make this decision or that as to the direction our church should go. But they also readily acknowledge that the real battles are won or lost on the local congregational level—and there, for better or for worse, the pastor usually carries (or at least markedly influences) the day.

Consequently, clergy who are both godly and competent can be tremendous forces for good. And conversely, those who are either ungodly or incompetent can wreak havoc.

This is particularly true when it comes to pastoral support of Adventist education. Decades ago it was considered de rigueur that pastors would wholeheartedly support our schools. And frankly, decades ago, that was much easier to do! As I pointed out earlier, Adventist members did indeed send their kids as a matter of course. The pastor's job was simple: Point the way to the school, and—with far fewer exceptions than today—members would enroll their children. But through the years things have changed dramatically in a number of ways. Let's consider some of them.

Believe it or not, Adventism is one of the best organizations in the world at winning unchurched people to Christ. (Russell Burrill, former professor at the Seventh-day Adventist Theological Seminary in Berrien Springs, Michigan, has suggested that the only group ahead of us is nondenominational churches.) Praise the Lord! However, one thing we've failed to reckon on is that success in this demographic has meant an increasing number of adult converts entering the pastoral workforce who have never attended Adventist or other Christian schools a day in their lives. "And yet look," some of those pastors say. "God still brought me through, and today, I'm even a minister!" Thus, they reason, why give support to Adventist education when such education is apparently not needed? (I vividly recall one of my pastoral colleagues in ministry who fit this description celebrating when at last the school his church supported died for lack of enrollment. He had made no secret of his disdain for Adventist education, and was openly jubilant when the school closed, freeing up money for "more important" tasks.)

Again, we praise God for bringing new people to our church. But it does not follow that simply because God made a minister out of someone who never attended our schools, Adventist education is irrelevant to becoming a Seventh-day Adventist Christian! Yet it is my impression that this is precisely the naive attitude of an increasing swath of Adventist ministers, and it is killing our schools.

To recommend against Adventist education because a comparatively few people became dedicated leaders in Adventism without its benefit is akin to urging that soldiers not wear body armor into battle—since, after all, some soldiers are never wounded, even after many tours of duty. Foolishness! The fact is that *public* education in the territory of the North American Division cannot intentionally disciple our children into Christ and Seventh-day Adventism, if for no other reason than that *it is illegal for it to do so.* And if a pastor—or anyone else, for that matter—suggests entrusting our children to such conditions instead of Adventist schools, they are at best naive and at worst incompetent in this most crucial area of discipleship!

Now if I seem overly harsh in this regard, let me remind you briefly of what I stated earlier. Non-Adventist teachers invariably influence—to a greater or lesser degree—our children to accept non-Adventist ways of living, even if those teachers don't say a word openly about it. Their very lives shout to our kids that as a teacher, they are someone who should be listened to, someone whose way of living should be copied. And yet those same teachers—regardless of their sincerity or kindness—almost certainly do not keep Sabbath, are too often morally relativistic (that is, they do not believe in the existence of objective truth), and are too often not preparing themselves or others for the soon return of Christ. *Children who thus go through public education and either remain passionate Adventists or become passionate Adventists are the exceptions, not the rule.* And God forbid that our pastors should undermine Adventist education by believing or propagating thinking to the contrary.

A second way that pastors show a lack of support for Adventist education has again to do with discipleship. I will not repeat what I have already mentioned earlier about the intentionality and effort required to make genuine Seventh-day Adventist disciples of Christ. But suffice it to say that if a pastor is either ignorant or incompetent in the area of discipleship, he or she will almost certainly not advocate Adventist education, for the same reasons previously mentioned that parents don't.

## The Pastoral Pressure Cooker

A third way that pastors fail to endorse Adventist education is perhaps more complex than the preceding two, but equally damaging. It has to do with the fact that many Adventist clergy today face incredible pressures to produce "results." What those results are expected to be varies.

For instance, in churches that do not take personal discipleship very seriously, many members believe that the pastor's main job is to serve them through personal visits, counseling, and general "pastoral" care. Ignoring the fact that these are Christian functions rather than pastoral functions (Adventist churches didn't even have local clergy in any sizable numbers until the 1920s and 1930s), such nonfunctioning members clamor for their ministers to produce the results of . . . attendance to their personal needs. Many (perhaps most) of our pastors give in to such individuals and seek to please them, as it tends to "keep peace" in the family.

Simultaneously, local conferences often have an additional set of expected results from the pastor. These may include tithe gains, membership accessions, special conference project promotion, or any number of other goals.

On top of this, there is still today a palpable push from the megachurch movement to have, well, a megachurch. Nonpastors may scoff at this (as do some pastors), but the pressure is real and appears to occur regardless of the size or location of a pastor's congregation. While Willow Creek and other high-profile churches have had some positive effects in Christendom, one of the perhaps unintended but oh-so-real consequences has been the assumption that if "those guys can do it, all local pastors can do it, too—and should!" So the pastor tries . . . and, for a variety of reasons, usually fails.

Unless they are dealt with appropriately, the consequences of having so many different and varied demands on the pastor can be dizzying. Many church members want a pastor who will coddle them, preach to them, attend to them, and care for them. Many conferences seek pastors who will generate tithe, more members, and special project support. And the general pastoral ethos would like a pastor who creates megachurches—or at least congregations that are radically and visibly growing in attendance. What's a pastor to do?

How about quit?

Archibald Hart, nationally recognized expert on adrenaline and stress, points out that the average pastoral career lasts just seven to 10 years in its entirety. Few indeed are the pastors who remain so for a lifetime (I've heard similar rumblings about teachers). But for those who don't quit, *many of them come to see Adventist education as yet another burden that sucks energy—and much-needed cash—away from their church.* If the school is embattled and struggling, the impression only intensifies. Why, the pastor asks, do I need to support yet another organization that is faltering when I can't seem to get done what's expected of me in the one I'm personally involved with?* Add to this the fact that local conferences rarely bother to inquire as to a pastor's conduct with regard to a local school, and we can begin to see why so many elementary schools, for instance, are closing their doors.

If we are to reverse the tide of decline in Adventist education, then the hearts and minds of many of our Adventist pastors will need changing as well. We'll touch on this more in chapter 19.

---

* Ironically, there is solid evidence to indicate that when pastors and their churches do commit to supporting Adventist education, those churches reap tangible benefits. A five-year study in the Michigan Conference revealed that all churches that were *not* constituents of a church school experienced, on average, a decrease in both tithe and membership every year of the study. But those churches that were constituents of a church school experienced, on average, an increase in tithe and membership every year of the study. How tragic that some pastors stifle the very thing that could help them achieve their (and their church's) goals! See "Gathering Greatness," *Adventist Review,* July 27, 2006, for more information.

# CHAPTER 5

# Poor Parenting

O uch! Now I've gone from preaching to meddling, haven't I? And thus I'm afraid I need to apologize in advance for this chapter, as it has the potential to rub some of you the wrong way. I'm sorry about that, and I mean it when I say that I'm not trying to insult anyone in what follows. But I also sincerely want to be of help to our educational system, and to do that, we have to deal with negative trends honestly so that we can find appropriate solutions that will work.

So let me put it out there: I believe that poor parenting has had a decided impact on Adventist (and no doubt other churches') educational efforts, and without at least a basic awareness of the impact this phenomenon has had on our schools, our attempted reversal of Adventist educational decline will be hampered.

The decline of the traditional family has received extensive documentation, and I won't bore you with more stats here. Suffice it to say that children raised in reasonably happy homes in which their biological parents are still married to each other are statistically sociological oddballs. Add to this a decline in competency in basic parenting skills on the part of a significant number of postmodern parents, and we have a simple but potent recipe for contributing to educational decline in our division and beyond.

A lack of basic parenting skills can manifest itself in the home in a number of ways. For instance, for a variety of reasons many parents lack either the drive or the knowledge to implement basic *consistency*. If a child disobeys a rule, for example, he or she should receive the appropriate consequences consistently with each infraction. But when parental responses vary too much, children tend to learn to be devious and disobedient. Moreover, parents need to provide consistency for their kids in other areas, such as spending time with them personally, as well as in establishing the simple practice of a regular daily routine for their kids to follow.

This, of course, is not rocket science. But without such consistency, children learn that life is meant to be unpredictable and erratic—and selfish indulgence is sure to follow. Without proper boundaries within which the family expects meals, chores, homework, etc., to occur, children inevitably become undisciplined and unmotivated to do the basic things required for success both spiritually and materially. When we factor in the unprecedented access most parents unwisely grant their children to popular media, it is easy to see why society as a whole appears to be morally sinking. Good parenting lifts a society, but poor parenting paves the way for a vast array of damage—including that on Adventist education.

## Long-Term Effects

When I have asked longtime Adventist teachers if anything has changed during the past 10-20 years as far as the caliber of students they deal with in their classroom, they have almost universally replied with an emphatic yes! Pressed as to what that difference is, the answers I've gotten center in three areas. 1. Students have less respect for them as a teacher. 2. Students are notably less motivated now to perform basic schoolwork functions (homework, projects, reading assignments, etc.). 3. Many more students have significant behavioral issues than in the past.

If these three observations are correct, then they easily explain a significant chunk of the demise of Adventist education—particularly at the secondary level, where life is further complicated by postpubescent adolescence. A single example may be sufficient to show why this is so.

Imagine that parents are having trouble with their teenage son. He's becoming decidedly rebellious and difficult to handle. Drug use, promiscuity, and other behavioral problems loom on the horizon. So the parents decide that what the student needs is to go off to an Adventist boarding academy. The parent turns in the application, the son gets accepted, and the parents have high hopes for the reformation of their prodigal.

At times, such an approach may be successful. But in my experience, the results more often turn out to be decidedly different. Particularly in a boarding school environment, extreme behaviorally challenged students often require more care than any staff outside of a reform school should reasonably be expected to provide. Moreover, boarding schools expect of students a measure of trustworthiness and self-motivation that frankly is foreign to a huge swath of the North American population. The faculty assumes that students will (brace yourselves) hold a basic job, show up for and study for classes and tests on their own initiative, and exhibit acceptable adherence to all school guidelines. But when young people lack sufficient training in such things for the first 14 years or so of their life, most boarding schools simply cannot turn that tide around and produce the model citizen their parents at home envision.

And note the other side of the coin. If the behaviorally challenged student is in an Adventist school made up mostly of well-behaved students who are fairly and consistently disciplined when needed, he might yet be sufficiently buffered to prevent widespread damage. However, if a school has a significant portion (in my estimation 5 percent or more) of its students that have significant behavioral problems, a number of potentially dangerous results are possible.

First and foremost, staff resources may get spread so thin that they cannot sufficiently deal with the problem students. Thus the problem students' bad behavior tends to thrive rather than be positively transformed. Second, staff morale can plummet, as seemingly student after student mocks them, skips classes, and is generally rebellious, giving the impression that the school (i.e., the staff) is failing. Third, because so much staff time gets taken up in dealing with problem students, other staff functions become neglected, and the quality of education the school offers can drop. And fourth, it doesn't take long for a school's reputation to tank badly when a significant number of students exhibit risky behaviors ranging from run-of-the mill sassing to drug and alcohol abuse. That institution can become known as a "party" school, in which kids do as they wish—which leads to an ironic situation: *The parents of the behaviorally challenged kids that contributed to that reputation may refuse to send their "partying" kids to that school in the future . . . because it's now a "party" school, and, after all, they're trying to get their child out of that.* The cycle thus comes full circle, and Adventist education suffers directly because of poor parenting in the home.

## Don't Hit "Send" Yet!

Now, before the hate e-mail starts to flow, let me hastily point out two things. First, I fully recognize that many parents face incredible challenges in raising their children—particularly single parents. The demands from their children often directly compete with their job and legitimate personal needs, and life can be exceedingly difficult all around. As a church, we must recognize this and do our best to support our families that face such heavy burdens.

But the fact that we recognize the burdens that parents bear does not minimize the impact that poor parenting has had on our schools. And unless we factor this phenomenon into our discussion, we will find ourselves trying to implement solutions that may fall short of the mark.

Second, some well-meaning proponents of Adventist education have stated that our schools ought to take anyone who wants to come, that "if a worldly student can't find help at our schools, then we are failing at our calling as Christians." While this may sound persuasive, it ultimately ignores both the magnitude of the problem and the abilities of most Adventist schools. The truth is that we live in the last days of earth's history. Society is more convoluted and evil now than it was even a generation ago. Our schools—except for those specifically set up to deal with such situations—are simply not equipped to handle sizable numbers of severely behaviorally challenged students. To ask otherwise well-trained and dedicated staff to cater to the dysfunctions of a sizable minority at the expense of the more stable majority is unfair not only to that staff but also to the students who truly do want to excel in life and behave accordingly. "Taking all comers" may appear to be a nifty and pious idea, but in practice it is a pipe dream that gives poor parenting skills the upper hand and leads to the detriment of all involved.

# CHAPTER 6

# The Success of the "-ism"s: Postmodernism, Secularism, and "Liberalism"

Pull out your dictionary. We're about to dive into the multisyllabic world of secular philosophy.

In chapter 1 I talked about how waning brand loyalty to Adventist institutions was only a symptom—not a root cause—of Adventist educational decline. It's now time to look at one of the main roots from which declining institutional loyalty springs: postmodernism.[1]

Postmodernism is the formal name for the way of thinking that says truth is relative to the observer. What's true for you may not be so for me, announces postmodern thought. Truth is thus migratory and dependent upon time and place for its determination. (One could more correctly define postmodernism as moral relativism or simply relativism, or, at its most extreme interpretation, as deconstructionism.) Thus postmodern thought sees the notion of absolute truth—that is, that something is true at all times and under all circumstances—as abhorrent and oppressive. The concept has some strong implications for Adventism in general and Adventist schools in particular.

First, postmodernism, when followed to its logical conclusion, regards any established institution as being inherently oppressive and confining. Institutions by definition endure over time. The reason for their survival is often that they have a strong core of beliefs that a group holds to be true. That is, they stand *for* some things and *against* some other things—a great sin (if there were such a thing) in postmodern thought!

Second, postmodernism marginalizes history itself, as history is (to state the obvious) unchanging. It is thus an unwelcome norm-setting influence that postmoderns often see as unnecessary and severely confining. So if you take an institution—say, Adventist education—and combine it with a strong sense of purpose as evidenced by history—the founding of Seventh-day Adventism, the three angels' messages, etc.—you have created the antithesis of postmodern thought. And for that, we are paying the price.

Consequently, we must see the 1960s and their countercultural and counterinstitutional fallout within the wider context of postmodernism. The results of that time period in particular have mushroomed today into deep-seated distrust of authority figures and the organizations they run. This even affects how North Americans spend their money and their time. And yes, the average consumer feels free to float from product to product, no longer tethered as our grandparents were by an enduring sense of brand or institutional loyalty.

In light of these developments, we Adventists have at times tried to put on a brave face and say that our members have largely escaped postmodern trends. But that's simply not true. It is a global trend, and anyone who lives on this planet—particular in its Western portions—finds themselves daily challenged to accept postmodernism's version of reality.

This is particularly true of schools, regardless of religious affiliation. For instance, our Catholic friends, operators of the largest private school system in the world, are facing tremendous challenges in their institutions. During the mid-1960s their elementary and secondary schools in the United States had an enrollment of nearly 5 million students. But today their approximately 7,800 elementary and secondary schools have approximately 2.4 million students—*less than half of what it was 40 years ago.* Why the decline? It is not because the United States has fewer Catholics. Rather, among the reasons given, one has been the "changing role of religion in the lives of American Catholics"—a nod to the inroads of postmodern thought.[2]

Adventist schools are suffering from the same malady, as is the wider Adventist Church. Commenting on the state of Christianity in the western world and the Adventist Church in particular, Harold Lee points out that "this new 'religious marketplace' is characterized by the privatization of religious belief and practice, marginalization of organized religion, relativization of all religious thought and conviction, and trivialization of religious teaching and practice. In this competitive environment, people participate in the church on their own terms, not on the church's terms. The church's influence declines."[3]

The impact of postmodernism on Adventist educational institutions should thus be obvious. Our schools are to stand for specific values and specific truths, and furthermore, they are to exist to inculcate those values and truths into their students. Can we wonder that enrollment is declining as postmodern thinking affects our members?

A third consequence that postmodernism has had on Adventist schools is that it has allowed into our schools (and our churches) its close cousin, secularism. I'll discuss this more in greater detail shortly. But I'll note now that we can roughly define secularism as the mode of thought that sees God as either removed from or optional to daily living. The individual (as the final arbiter of what constitutes "truth"), not God, determines how he or she should live. Morality predictably declines in such a mindset, as the human proclivity to do evil finds itself set free to choose one's path. Again, more on this shortly.

## The "Conservative"-"Liberal" Divide

A fourth impact of postmodernism on Adventist schools concerns "liberalism." No, I am not saying that "liberal" Adventists are direct products of postmodern thought. But I do believe that the current wave of "liberalism" in the Adventist Church has indeed been fed and spurred on by postmodern thought, and as such demands a closer look.

You'll recall that earlier I spoke of the passion for "conservative" Adventism as being crucial to the health of our schools. Now it's time to live dangerously again by attempting to describe what a "conservative Adventist"—versus a "liberal Adventist"—is. Why? Because I believe the "conservative"-"liberal" divide goes a long way toward explaining the demise of Adventist education. So let's take a look at these two groups— fully realizing that defining them exactly for all cases is impossible. (And please note: If you find the following descriptions overly challenging or just plain offensive, please don't trash this book until you've read the special note to "liberal" and "conservative" Adventists at the end of this chapter.)

Let's look at "conservatives" first. In my estimation, to be a "conservative" Adventist today means that you passionately live out the unique mission of the Adventist Church—that is, you are a loving and lovable Christian who exemplifies what Adventism teaches. You are dedicated to what it stands for. Thus you keep the Sabbath holy by communing with Christ and not working, buying, or selling on that day; you do your best to take care of your body; you believe in and live out the sanctuary and other Adventist doctrines; you believe that Ellen White was a true prophet of God and take her writings seriously; and you are cautious in exposing yourself and your children to worldly media and other influences. As a result, your greatest challenges may be twofold: (1) to remember that God's love is the spring of all truly good behavior; and (2) not to slam liberal Adventists for not being like you.

On the other hand, to be a "liberal" Adventist means, in my opinion, that you also strive to be a loving and lovable Christian. But the notion of Adventism having a unique mission to carry out in the world seems troubling and hauntingly elitist. Moreover, Sabbathkeeping may be determined more by personal preference than enduring principle, and working, buying, and selling on that day may be acceptable to you in a number of ways (going out to eat, buying gas and a measure of groceries, for example). Maintaining your health is a good thing, but not necessarily a spiritual thing. You may consider the sanctuary doctrine as somewhat cumbersome and at least fuzzy, while other doctrines, particularly ones in which Adventism differs from other faiths, you prefer to discuss more as helpful options for the world than as "thus saith the Lord"s. Ellen White's value is questionable. Her writings, if read at all, are considered to be more a commentary on the era in which she lived than anything applicable to the church today. And as for avoiding worldly influences, as a liberal Adventist you shun them, too—though your definition of what constitutes "worldly" may be much more narrow than a conservative Adventist's would be. Consequently, your greatest challenges may also be twofold: (1) to realize that those who truly love God will crave and joyfully pursue personal obedience to His specific commands; and (2) yes, not to slam conservative Adventists for not being like you.

I hope the above descriptions have not been needlessly offensive. But if you are upset, please continue to read, because the conservative/liberal divide is, in my opinion, only widening and is separating our church in such a way that is catastrophic in a number of areas, including Adventist education.

Which brings us to a story—one painted with admittedly broad brushstrokes and oversimplifications, but hopefully helpful nonetheless.

During the 1960s and 1970s tremendous changes swept our country—and our church. The benevolent but top-down church leadership style of the 1950s, once unquestioningly accepted as appropriate, began to face heavy challenges (along with almost every other form of authority) in the 1960s from postmodern thought. Well-intended but at times overzealous Adventist hard-liners, once solidly in control of church politics, began to lose their grip (though in truth that loss of control traced its roots all the way back to the 1920s when Christianity in general debated the notion of fundamentalism and its role in the church).

The 1970s and 1980s (and even, in a few areas, the early 1990s) proved to be the zenith of Adventist education as far as elementary and secondary school enrollment was concerned.[4] (Our colleges, however, were hitting new lows in enrollment[5]—an interesting phenomenon for another study.) In part this resulted from Adventist baby boomers producing sizable numbers of children with which to populate our schools, and by the fact that we had inertia on our side: Adventist families for generation after generation sent their children to Adventist schools. Academies with 300 or even 400-plus students became common in North America. Life appeared to be good.

Then, in the early and mid-1980s, overall enrollment in Adventist primary and secondary schools across the division began to wane—and with it, the perceived good times. Some pointed to a generational blip as the cause of our woes—that is, that we were experiencing the natural rise and fall of birth rates between successive generations. However, while that may have accounted in part for our declining enrollment, a generational blip could not explain a disturbing corollary—namely, that not only were fewer and fewer students attending our schools, but also that fewer and fewer Adventists *wanted* to send their kids to them. A shift not only in numbers but in *attitude* had mysteriously appeared, confounding school boards and staff across the country.

What had gone wrong?

Several things, some of which we've already discussed. But with particular regard to our current topic, a fair slice of the apathy (and sometimes hostility) about enrolling children in Adventist schools came from *the postmodernism-fueled conservative-liberal debate as to what Adventism—and by extension Adventist education—should be like.* In this case, liberalism prevailed, and it was—and is—causing a continuing decline in enrollment in Adventist schools.

I realize that's a bold and potentially inflammatory statement. But before liberal Adventists dismiss me out of hand, please understand the economics of the Adventist lifestyle.

Almost any experienced school administrator will tell you that conservative Adventism has (with few exceptions) been the mainstay of Adventist education at the elementary and secondary level. This is not to say that liberal Adventists never sent or do not send their children to Adventist schools—far from it. However, in my experience, they have generally done so in considerably fewer numbers than conservatives have (with the possible exceptions of a few of our boarding academies in the 1980s and early 1990s). Why? Several reasons may exist. But certainly at the top of the list is that generally, liberal Adventists perceive the issues of Adventist uniqueness, Sabbathkeeping, entertainment, healthful living, and so forth to be topics exceedingly open to interpretation and rarely subject to a clear "thus saith the Lord." As a result, they are often comfortable in sending their kids to another Christian school that is closer to home or is less expensive, or in enrolling them in a quality public school.

Conservative Adventists, on the other hand, want very much to have their children embrace the unique mission of Adventism as well as the specifics of the Adventist lifestyle. They view Adventist schools as bona fide propagators of Adventism, as centers of learning that will successfully perpetuate the Adventist faith. Certainly, such parents also desire for their children to embrace freedom of inquiry, to learn to ask questions, and to engage wisely and freely with those holding views different from their own. But they want the particulars of Adventism's uniqueness concurrently, intelligently, and passionately promoted—a service for which they will pay high amounts of money to enroll their children in schools that will do precisely that.

Which of course leads to a sore point of contention today. Could it be that too many of our schools—particularly at the secondary and college levels—have become too liberal for conservatives to send their kids to, and— notice carefully—too *liberal for liberals to enroll their kids in, as well?*

Let's explore how this might be true by taking some specific examples from Adventist school campus life. Part of the fallout from the 1960s and 1970s was a questioning of the importance of many of Adventism's traditional taboos on boarding academy campuses and the corresponding inroads of secularism. This was particularly true with regard to media and interpersonal social relations. For instance, in the 1980s and even on into the early 1990s most of our academies prohibited radios or TVs in dorm rooms. Schools also carefully regulated driving privileges to keep students from taking other students off campus at inappropriate times or for inappropriate reasons. And as for dating policies, academies either heavily restricted dating (and certainly physical contact) or banned it altogether.

By the mid-to-late 1990s, however, many educational institutions had made substantial shifts in these areas, largely in response to either liberal Adventist parents requesting such changes or liberal Adventist staff mandating them themselves. For example, while there were exceptions, schools increasingly allowed students to have a variety of media in their rooms (Walkmans, CD/DVD players, TVs, and today, iPods, etc.), making the monitoring of the content being viewed/listened to difficult. Students could also have personal computers, giving them the ability to listen to and view questionable music and material. Driving privileges expanded beyond previous norms, allowing unsupervised town trips. And as for dating, school administrations not only more widely allowed it but even encouraged it, admonishing students to "touch only this much [hugs, hand-holding, back rubs, etc.] and no more."

At this point I need to make something abundantly clear. Some of you are anticipating that I see the relaxing of such social and media use policies as detrimental to our schools. You are correct. However, it is *not* the relaxing of such policies *in and of itself* that I believe has been harmful, but rather doing so *without commensurate efforts to educate our students on how to deal with their newfound freedoms.* In other words, too often it appears that we granted new opportunities in our schools but neglected to teach our students how to make wise choices about (for instance) what music to listen to or what DVDs to watch. Sure, we may have discussed the topics in Bible class. But how often was that (1) an isolated, once-or-twice-a-year occurrence and thus (2) woefully inadequate at monitoring throughout the rest of the year whether or not a student was actually mature enough in their faith to make good media and social decisions? When it comes to our students in their formative years, an easing of social and media use policies without proper ongoing instruction and accountability for how to deal with those new freedoms is a recipe for disaster.

Consequently, in the eyes of conservatives (and, to be fair, a number of moderate liberals), the quality of campus life predictably deteriorated. Informed Adventists point out that with puberty happening statistically earlier and intellectual maturity coming statistically later—to say nothing of the amazing availability through the media of all manner of sexually explicit material—many boarding academy students today are more poised to fall into at-risk behaviors than perhaps ever before. The relaxing of behavioral standards at our boarding school campuses has formed in some parents' minds a picture of the perfect storm: immature students with easy access to suggestive music, pornography, and fellow students' bodies.

Add to this the relaxing—again, often at the urging of liberal Adventists—of a number of other standards, and the picture for many conservative parents becomes even bleaker. For instance, Sabbath observance—the marking of its coming and going, the refraining from travel for sporting or other secular events on Sabbath, buying and selling on Sabbath—has become more casual in many of our schools. And the list could go on.

All of this is to say that liberal Adventists, regardless of the rightness or wrongness of their desires, have succeeded in "liberalizing" many Adventist schools. And the results are surprising. Not only will an increasing number of conservative Adventists no longer send their students to our boarding academies, *but neither will more and more liberal Adventists. After all, why pay thousands of dollars to send your child to a school that is now no longer substantially different from the average Christian school—or the local public school—down the street?* Liberal Adventists already had tendencies toward enrolling their kids in non-Adventist schools, and the liberalizing of some of our Adventist schools has only increased that pattern. The irony is obvious: The very group that pushed for the liberalization of our schools will now support them even less because they're, well, too liberal!

And thus the inroads of postmodernism, secularism, and liberalism help explain the current decline in Adventist education.

## A Special Note to "Conservative" and "Liberal" Adventists

Upon reviewing the manuscript for this book, a friend of mine with long experience at many levels of church governance (and whose opinion I greatly respect) nearly choked when he read this chapter. Prior to this point in the book he had merely written brief notes in the margins. But pages 42 and 43 in particular occasioned an entire page of heated response! Here's part of what he said:

"You portray conservatives as gentle, kindhearted preservers of all that is good and liberals as dangerous in both loose thinking and living. I grew up in the days that you refer to and served as youth leader . . . during those days. I remember the conservatives as mean-spirited, hardheaded, unbending people who sought to control behavior rather than teach responsible decision-making. They tried to forbid the use of technology—film, TV, radio, recordings, digital equipment—rather than use them wisely. In the process they managed to drive young people in large numbers from our schools and the church. . . . [On the other hand,] I remember liberals as those who sought to help young people learn to live in the real world and make wise moral decisions. They were nice to live with."

My friend makes a good point, one that compels me to make some clarifications.

1. *I believe the definitions of "liberal" and "conservative" are different today than they were 30 years ago—maybe even 10 years ago.* As I mentioned before, that's the problem with trying to define the terms today. Circumstances and people change. And chances are that if for some reason the Lord tarries for a number of years more, the definitions of the terms I offer today will later on be outmoded.

2. *If I were alive and ministering during the time my friend was, I hope that I would have been classified as a liberal.* We've all heard the stories from days gone by when "conservative" meant—and honestly so—someone who was so committed to their "spiritual" ideas that they were a threat to themselves and anyone they came in contact with. Their idea of a "good time" was scanning others for even the smallest sign of sin and purifying (read "persecuting") them accordingly. Far from being a reason for rejoicing, their commitment to God was a heavy burden that spiritually speaking seemed to make them have more in common with the Grinch than with Christ.

History is helpful in illustrating this phenomenon. In Jesus' day the Pharisees were the conservatives and Jesus the long-haired rat pack, unkempt (not a lot of campgrounds with showers in Jesus' day) and liberal. How we needed (and need) His brand of liberalism! In the sixteenth century the established church was the conservative voice and Martin Luther the stubborn, obstinate, and ultimately liberating liberal. Again, how the world needed Lutheran liberalism! And during the 1950s through the 1980s many Adventists were suffocatingly conservative—measuring dress lengths to the millimeter, Big

Brother-ing relationships, and melting Heritage Singers records with gusto. And thankfully, into that prison cell came some well-balanced, well-reasoned, and trustworthy liberals who helped to turn the tide. And yes, how we needed their liberalism! It would have been an honor to be a liberal along with my friend during his years of service.

3. *The liberal victories of 30 years ago have been misappropriated and abused today.* Again, let me paint with broad, overly general brushstrokes and say that, to my thinking, many liberals of the present day have significantly altered the blessings that intelligent liberals brought to the church during the past three decades. Whereas before liberals such as my friend were pushing for a thinking approach to Adventist values—and, dare I say it, an approach more favored by Ellen White, who nearly always saw the word "conservative" in a negative light—today, I perceive many liberal Adventists seeking to dismiss the importance of Adventist values out of hand, at times completely, without investigation and without discussion. And while liberals such as my friend wanted to ask uncomfortable questions about the Adventist lifestyle in the hopes of anchoring it more firmly in the Bible, liberals today often seem to have already decided that the Adventist lifestyle is mere culture and thus without basis at all in Scripture. Previously liberals such as my friend sought to replace mindless adherence to rules with solid, faithful reasoning abilities. Today, though, too many liberals seek to replace rules . . . with nothing in particular.

The pendulum has swung too far. The legitimate gains that such liberals as my friend achieved in the past have been abused. Which leads me to a final point.

4. *The kind of conservatism that the Adventist Church needs today is joyful, open-minded, and free—that is, centered in Christ. It is passionate about Adventist core beliefs, but is free from the tyranny of legalism.* If you're a conservative Adventist and you're not joyful in Jesus, you may want to check your spiritual pulse. Are you still breathing? Or have you swung the pendulum dangerously close to the conservative sins of the past?

I remember from a number of years ago the first time that someone told me I was a conservative Adventist. *I am not,* I thought. *I enjoy living.* Now I see that indeed, I am, currently, a "conservative" Adventist. But not in the vein of the Heritage Singers-hating years gone by. Instead, I crave revival in my church, not through a mindless conservatism from the past or the at-times directionless and chaotic liberalism of the present, but rather through a passionate recognition of the joyful, prophetic calling that God has given to the Adventist Church for my and countless others' fulfillment.

That's what I mean when I call for being a "conservative" Adventist.

---

[1] After reading this chapter, those of you who keep up with Western cultural trends may wish that I had included a segment on post-postmodernism, the emerging normative philosophy that appears to be rapidly taking postmodernity to its logical—and potentially catastrophic—end. However, because post-postmodernism is still relatively young and because postmodernism has done the lion's share of damage to Adventist education, I focus solely on the latter rather than the former in this chapter. But make no mistake: post-postmodernism is sufficiently hostile to Christian belief that it may just provide Adventist education with its greatest challenge—or, if navigated correctly, its finest hour.

[2] Reported at *www.adventistreview.org/article,php?id=988#2* (from an article by Daniel Burke, Religions News Service).

[3] H. Lee, "Church Structure in 2025."

[4] Relevant statistics are available from the NAD Office of Education.

[5] See D. Malcolm Maxwell, "The Future of SDA Higher Education: A North American College President's Perspective," *Journal of Adventist Education* 47, no. 5 (Summer 1985): 12.

# CHAPTER 7

# Poor-Quality Schools

No, not all our schools are poor quality! Far from it. But enough are that we must consider them a significant part of the challenge facing Adventist education.

I hope that by now it is clear that many of the reasons for the current crisis in Adventist education lie outside of Adventist education proper. But that is not to say (as this chapter will seek to illustrate) that our schools themselves bear no responsibility for the decline, for they certainly do. Perhaps we could describe the relationship between the church and the school in the following manner: A great deal of the time our schools, by and large, have come to reflect, rather than necessarily determine, what their constituents are looking for. But once they successfully reflect the desires of their constituent churches in their school programs, they also serve to—with every graduate—propagate and deepen the strengths and flaws of those churches in the next generation of Adventists. Thus both the church and the school share responsibility for our educational decline, and both must participate in resuscitative efforts if we are to climb back to health.

So what have been some of our schools' contributions to Adventist educational decline? What are some of the quality concerns that have increasingly kept parents from enrolling their children in our educational institutions in general?

## Quality Concern 1:
## Lack of Passion for the Primary Goal of Adventist Education

What should be the fundamental purpose of an Adventist school?

What should be at the top of every staff member's list of things to do first?

Ask some Adventists, and they'll cite proper academic instruction as being the primary objective. Others, more widely read, will tell you that the ultimate purpose of our schools is either to prepare students for the mission of the church or to foster proper character development—two very worthy goals that should be of exceedingly great importance to any Adventist school.

But are any of these to be the *primary* goal of Adventist schools?

No. At least not according to some pretty on-the-ball experts in Adventist education.

Ellen White, in her book *Education* (a good read, by the way, and a great place to find solutions to our current ills) reveals clearly what the fundamental intent of Adventist education is. And while I could comment on it myself, I think my former seminary professor George Knight put it best in his book *Myths in Adventism*. The following quotation is a lengthy one, but his analysis is so spot-on that it deserves ample space.

"Why have Seventh-day Adventist schools? Why do Adventists spend millions of dollars each year to support approximately five thousand schools around the world when free public education is often available? How can we justify such expenditures in the light of the other pressing needs of the church and the world that it serves? The answer to such questions has of necessity a link to the purpose of Adventist education. If Adventist schools serve a sufficiently distinctive and important purpose, the achievement of that purpose is worth their cost. Establishing and clearly understanding the true object of Christian education is therefore crucial to the continued support and operation of Adventist schools. In fact, the most important educational understanding a Christian can arrive at is related to the purposes, aims, and goals of education. . . .

"Ellen White highlighted the crucial nature of educational aims and purposes when she wrote that '*by a misconception of the true nature and object of education, many have been led into serious and even fatal errors.*'—*Counsels to Parents, Teachers, and Students*, p. 49. (Italics supplied.) Her powerful statement implies that for many people a mistaken notion of educational aims has been eternally fatal. 'Such a mistake is made,' she added, 'when the regulation of the heart or the establishment of principles is neglected in the effort to secure intellectual culture, or when eternal interests are overlooked in the eager desire for temporal advantage.'—*Ibid.* It is easy to see that she disqualifies both intellectual learning and job preparation as the primary goals of education. . . . What, then, we might ask, is the real objective of Christian education? . . .

"In the passage that undergirds her entire philosophy of education, Ellen White pointed out that if we are to comprehend the meaning and goal of education we will have to understand four things about man: (1) his original nature, (2) the purpose of God in creating him, (3) the change that took place in the human condition at the Fall, and (4) God's plan for yet fulfilling His purpose in the education of the human race (*Education*, pp. 14, 15).

"She then went on to explain the four items. First, man was created in the image of God. Second, mankind was to reveal ever more fully God's image by continual development throughout eternity. Third, disobedience badly damaged, but did not destroy, the image in its mental, physical, and spiritual aspects. Man's disobedience also brought death. Fourth, God did not turn His back on man in his hopeless condition; He still intended to fulfill His purpose for the human race by restoring His image in man through the plan of salvation. Education is one of God's redemptive and restorative agencies. Therefore, indicated Mrs. White, the primary purpose of education is to lead students to God for redemption (*ibid.*, pp. 15, 16).

"Scripture presents the same picture. Central to an understanding of the Bible is man's fall in Genesis 3. Here is one of the most crucial chapters in the Bible. Neither Scripture nor daily experience makes sense if we explain away as legend the first three chapters of Genesis. According to Genesis, God created humanity in His image and likeness—an exalted state (Gen. 1:26, 27). Man, however, rejected God and chose his own way. As a result, he became alienated and separated from God (chap. 3:8-10), his fellowman (verses 11, 12), his own self (verse 13), and the natural world (verses 17-19). Separating himself from the source of life, he became subject to death (chaps. 2:17; 3:19). Man had become hopeless and *lost* in the fullest sense of the word.

"The lostness of man provides the purpose of Christian education. *Man's greatest need is to become 'unlost.'* Thus Jesus claimed that He came 'to seek and to save that which was lost' (Luke 19:10, KJV). Such seeking and saving is the theme of the Bible from Genesis 3 to Revelation 20. The message of the Bible from the Fall to the restoration of Eden in Revelation 21 is the story of how God, through teachers, prophets, patriarchs, preachers, symbolic services, and a host of other means, has been attempting to rescue man from his lostness. We must see Christian education in this context. 'In the highest sense,' penned Ellen White, 'the work of education and the work of redemption are one' because both build directly upon Jesus Christ. *To lead the student into a saving relationship with Jesus Christ 'should be the teacher's first effort and his constant aim'* (ibid., p. 30; italics supplied). Here is education's highest and primary goal. . . .

"Christian education is the only education that can meet man's deepest needs, because only Christian educators understand the core of the human problem. The redemptive aim of Christian education is what makes it Christian. The primary aim of Christian education in the school, the home, and the church is to lead young people into a saving relationship with Jesus Christ. This heals the principal alienation of Genesis 3—that between man and God. And the healing of the God/man relationship sets the stage for the removal of man's other basic alienations. Education is a part of God's great plan of redemption, or atonement. The role of education is to help bring man back to at-one-ness with God, his fellowman, his own self, and the natural world. The whole message of the Bible points forward to the day when the work of restoration will be complete and the Edenic condition will be restored in the realm of nature because of the healing of man's manifold lostness (Revelation 21, 22; Isa. 11:6-9; 35). . . .

"The student's greatest need, then, is for a spiritual rebirth that places God at the center of his existence. Paul noted that such renewal is a daily experience, and Jesus taught that the Holy Spirit accomplishes the transformation (1 Cor. 15:31; John 3:5). Christian education can never take place, we must emphasize, without the dynamic power of the Holy Spirit.

"Mrs. White wrote that the 'all-important thing' in education 'should be the conversion' of the students (*Fundamentals of Christian Education*, p. 436). *It is upon the foundation of the new birth experience that Christian education can proceed with its other aims and purposes. If it fails at this foundational and primary point, it has failed entirely.*"[1]

Who would've guessed?

*At its core, Adventism education is indeed all about Jesus!* He is the student's Friend, Master, Comforter, and yes, Redeemer. To convert students that they might know Him and be with Him is the primary purpose of every genuinely Adventist school. And even after conversion, our unique doctrines are not different just for their own sake, but rather are divine pathways that lead into ever-deeper communion with Jesus Christ. To know Christ is the definition of salvation (John 17:3). How could an Adventist school have any primary goal other than union with the Author of our salvation?

Yet such deviations have happened—again and again. Academics, music, sports, or other important but definitely secondary things have crowded out this primary drive for the salvation of students. Think carefully: What is the Adventist school near you known *most* for? Superior academic studies? A great varsity basketball team? Really nice facilities? A diverse student body? Advanced study opportunities? Great music instruction programs? If so, that school may well have missed the mark God intended for it to hit squarely. But if that school that has a reputation for the fact that *Jesus Christ is found there*, then the principal, staff, and teachers are indeed putting the right things first.

It should thus go without saying that if an Adventist school is not first and foremost seeking to establish their students in a personal, saving relationship with Christ, the blessing that those schools receive from God will be less than it otherwise would.

Now, I realize that that notion—of God withholding His blessing because of our behavior—troubles some of us. But let us consider carefully: Why would it be otherwise? Why would God mindlessly pour out His Holy Spirit on anything that didn't put His agenda at the top of its list? Pre-Christian, Christian, and even Adventist history are replete with example after example of God holding back His full blessings from those who refuse to put Him first. Are we so naive as to think that our schools today will be an exception to that rule? I pray not. Let us return the issue of our students' spirituality to the top of the list, for our lack of emphasis on this primary goal explains much of Adventist education's decline.

## Quality Concern 2:
## Lack of Passion for Things Uniquely Adventist

I still remember the conversation vividly. "The Adventist school is excellent!" the *non*-Adventist mother of two attending students said. "I recommend it to my [non-Adventist] friends whenever I get the chance. And when they question the fact that it's an Adventist school, I assure them that there's nothing offensive that's ever taught there and that they don't need to worry about their kids being made into Adventists."

Her words almost made me choke. On the one hand, I was grateful that this non-Adventist Christian woman had sent her kids to an Adventist institution. On the other, it was obvious from her statement that the school was failing in a very important area—making *Adventist* disciples of Christ out of its students.

Let me hasten to point out that I am not saying that Adventism in its entirety is inherently offensive, nor that it should be. Far from it! I have spent hundreds and hundreds of hours with non-Adventist people, both other Christians and many, many HPAAs (hard-core pagans, atheists, and agnostics). I have planted a church aimed specifically at such people, and have labored long to see them come to Christ. And after years of doing so, I've reached at least one conclusion: Adventism absolutely *rocks* for a whole bunch of those people! (For those of you needing interpretation of that last sentence, that means that these people often really, really like Adventism.)

*And* if what Adventists are preaching or teaching isn't offensive to at least *some* of the people, we're probably not presenting Bible truth—and thus Adventism—correctly.

To say otherwise is simply naive. Jesus Christ—who, I think it's safe to say, knew a thing or two about how to present Bible truth—was ultimately crucified for offending people with it. The Master Teacher was at times masterly offensive!

That is why Christianity has always been a fighting religion. It is and always will be offensive to those who think themselves self-sufficient and self-righteous *regardless of how kindly and lovingly we present Christianity*. The Holy Spirit Himself pointed out that Christ was "a stone that causes men to stumble and a rock that makes them fall" (1 Peter 2:8). Genuine biblical truth always brings with it a measure of pain as the Spirit convicts of sin and presses for reform. Salvation and Adventism are serious business—and seriously offensive to some of the people all of the time.

The point is this: Could it be that our schools are in dire straits in part because we're too shy about who we really are? As mentioned earlier, could it be that God has withdrawn His blessing from any particular Adventist school in direct measure to its unwillingness to be passionately Seventh-day Adventist? It is no accident that, all other things being equal, secondary schools and colleges in particular that are perceived as being "more conservative" are generally doing more business today than those regarded as being "more liberal"—and more often than not, being "more conservative" means that the particular school is more openly Adventist in its emphases, curriculum, and campus life. Add to this the fact that conservative Adventism has always been the mainstay of Adventist education, and you have one of the top keys to reviving Adventist education—becoming passionately and openly Adventist!

I must reiterate that we should *never* go out of our way to offend someone intentionally. Bashing people with the Bible and its truths is not only counterproductive but also sinful. But the simple fact still remains: *Our schools, when they are faithful to their calling, will and should disturb some people simply because we kindly teach unpopular and forgotten truths.* If we are not presenting them, if our schools are so unloving and banal and wimpy that they water down our unique message so that "no one will be offended" and so that we'll "attract more non-Adventists," the sooner we put a padlock on the doors and a For Sale sign on the lawn, the better. Such "Adventist" schools are mockeries to God, the very one who created this Advent movement to help prepare the world for the second coming of Christ and to whom we are unfaithful stewards if we refuse to proclaim that which He has commanded us. How can we possibly lay claim to the title "Seventh-day Adventist school" if we are not faithfully—even passionately—striving with all our might to prepare students to be Christ-followers who are Adventist missionaries in whatever vocation they choose? Have we forgotten the pronouncement that Jesus made long ago, one that still carries every ounce of power today?

"Not everyone who says to me, 'Lord, Lord,' will enter the kingdom of heaven, *but only he who does the will of my Father who is in heaven.* Many will say to me on that day, 'Lord, Lord, did we not prophesy in your name, and in your name drove out demons and perform many miracles?' Then I will tell them plainly, 'I never knew you. Away from me, you evildoers!' " (Matt. 7:21-23).

God forbid that any of our schools should ever hear such a pronouncement! But on our current course it is possible that many of them will unless substantive and tangible changes in focus, curriculum, and campus life take place. We are called to be Adventist schools—nothing less—and God will not account us faithful until we fulfill that calling (more on what that means in part four).

## Quality Concern 3:
## Poor School Leadership and Administration

We have already addressed the effect of poor pastoral leadership on Adventist education. Now let's turn to the dicey subject of poor leadership and administration within the Adventist school itself.

I say "dicey" because of the possibility that any principal or lead educator reading this section may take offense at what I'm going to say. So let me state straight off that with very few exceptions, the school administrators that I have met—be they local or conference—have been courteous, kind, and (to put it mildly) very dedicated to seeing Adventist education flourish. Yet nearly to a person, the schools they manage are not thriving, but experiencing decline and demise (and note: we could say the same thing about many, many *pastors* and their *churches* but that's another book for another day). Why isn't their dedication translating into reform and revival of the Adventist school? The answer may not be that they aren't good leaders, but rather that they are the wrong *kind* of leaders.

How's that for vague?

Let's elucidate by looking at things from the perspective of an elementary or secondary Adventist school principal. Twenty or 30 years ago, leading our schools was easier in some key ways—if for no other reason than that you generally didn't have to worry about perpetually declining enrollment. We were often flush with students, and the panic of possibly closing the school doors wasn't even on the horizon. To make an analogy, it's as though our schools were akin to cruise ships, and to run them effectively a principal needed to lead like a cruise ship captain. Major changes in course, for instance, were able to be (and probably, most of the time, should have been) made slowly and carefully. And one could largely ignore major "storms," because although they were unpleasant to both captain and crew, the "boat" was so big that it could ride out even the roughest of seas through sheer inertia.

Moreover, the pomp and grandeur of the cruise ship was impressive, and buoyed up (did I say that?) the reputation of the captain—even if his or her skill level was not top shelf. For instance, the ceremonies connected with the arrival of the "ship" in any new "port" (graduation, for instance) were lavish affairs, with lots of "passengers" "disembarking" to grand music and much hubbub. It was good to be captain under such conditions.

Which were all too short-lived. Today such generously endowed "cruise ships" are largely things of the past. Academies that have capacities for 300-500 students regularly host half that or less, or have simply shut their doors altogether. Picture an old cruise ship docked at a port, long since having ceased to go to sea, decks rusting, covered with barnacles at the water line, permanently moored, with just enough "passengers" to keep the thing above water . . . for the moment. Next year? Well, let's just say no one is terribly optimistic. Perhaps those who previously sailed on the ship (alumnae) will find it in their wallets to keep the thing afloat for another year. But even they are getting tired of bailing the boat out of trouble.

So what to do?

Before we answer that, let's be clear on how we've answered that question *functionally* speaking. In other words, let's not look on what we say, but rather on what we've actually *done* when we've tried to move our schools back into health. What actions have we taken?

Well, generally, we've hired . . . more cruise ship captains. After all, who else would know better how to run a cruise ship than a cruise ship captain? And they are usually courteous, kind, and dedicated. And they work hard.

And the ship still sinks.

Here's the truth about Adventist schools: You can have a strong commitment to win souls to Christ and a strong commitment to being faithful to Adventism's calling and *still* have to close the doors of a school *unless you have the right kind of leadership at the helm of the individual school.* And notice I didn't say "nice leadership" or "kind leadership" or "dedicated leadership," as indispensable as such traits are. I specifically said the *right kind* of leadership—that is what will win the day.

And what manner of leadership is that?

I admit I'm getting a little bit ahead of myself here, as the bulk of the discussion on how to bring Adventist education back to health is in part four. But here's a brief preview. To continue our oceangoing metaphor, we no longer need cruise ship captains at the helm of our "ships." *Instead, we need destroyer captains.*

A destroyer in the U.S. Navy, for instance, is a ship considerably smaller, more agile, and more efficiently run than any cruise ship would ever desire to be. Heavily armed to face any enemy, it is highly maneuverable. And it wastes no space on unnecessary amenities, since the vessel is intensely focused on carrying out its primary mission.

Obviously, such a ship requires an entirely different skill and mind-set of its captain than does its cruise ship counterpart. For one thing, while both types of captain are concerned about the well-being of their crew and passengers, the destroyer captain is far more aware of the intensity of opposition they might face on any given day—and consequently, such officers of necessity make decisions faster and with greater precision. Course corrections to adapt to changing conditions occur as quickly and effectively as possible. Egotism is out, as the importance of both the ship's occupants' well-being and the accomplishment of the mission are greater than the destroyer captain's personal reputation. When an enemy threatens—or when the destroyer must attack an enemy first—the captain has already made certain that crew members are well-drilled in what to do, and where, how, and when. In short, destroyer captains bring a level of intensity, decisiveness, and vision to their post that would blow the portholes right out of their cruise ship captain counterparts.

Which brings us to what I find to be a profound question: *If you were going to war, which captain would you want, and on which ship?*

We are at war! The days of cruising serenely through the waters of this world with graceful slowness and delightful lethargy are gone. And no, there is not a surplus of openings for cruise ship captains. We instead desperately need destroyer captains who not only have the ability to lead decisively and effectively in times of war, but also—get this—*can take our old cruise liners and, wherever appropriate, reshape them into destroyers.*

All right, toss the metaphors aside for a moment. Today one of our greatest needs is for principals, lead teachers, and school administrators that are top-notch directors of change. Any school that's declining and that still insists on hiring leaders that either refuse or are unable to recognize the seriousness of the times that we live in and lead accordingly is asking to close its doors. We need leadership that is unafraid to make the hard decisions—and quickly when necessary—concerning corrective changes in staffing, curriculum, and campus life. School administrators today must establish a culture of accountability, particularly among staff members, that holds them responsible for the quality of both their instruction and their spiritual influence at the school. (Obviously, this cries out for forward-thinking and supportive school boards, as well. More on that, too, in part four, as well as dealing with the challenges of recruiting and/or developing good leaders for our schools.)

Adventist education can rise again, but it will take transitional leadership, leaders with full dedication to Christ and Adventism *and* who possess strong vision for renewal and the courage to risk all that's necessary to see a school return to health. (We'll talk about how to obtain this type of leadership in chapters 12 and 19.) Barring this type of leadership, it will most likely continue to be a dark day "at sea" in Adventist education.

## Quality Concern 4:
## Are We Academically Adequate?

We used to hear that Adventist school students consistently performed better on standardized testing than their public school counterparts. A conclusion based on solid research, it thus became a source of considerable pride within the Adventist community.

But is this boast still justifiable? The short answer is: probably so! As I write this, CognitiveGenesis, a division-wide study of our students' academic performance, is into its second year, and the preliminary results are most encouraging.[2] It does indeed appear that the old blanket statement still stands firm: Adventist school students consistently outperform their public school counterparts in nearly every academic area, regardless of size, location, or enrollment. Well done, teachers and staff!

So in the face of this truly good news, why do I still list academics as a potential (and let me emphasize that word "potential") quality concern? For two reasons.

1. Even if the completed CognitiveGenesis report comes back with comparatively glowing statistics, *our enrollment is still declining and only a minority of eligible students are attending our schools.* This presents a rather ominous proposition. It is possible that we have been and are academically superior across the board compared to public schools, and yet we are still losing students to the public school system!

If that is true, there are relatively few possible explanations for the phenomenon. But we will consider three of them. First, it may be that most Adventist parents don't know about the academic prowess of our schools, and thus we need to market to them heavily in this regard. Second, it may be that most Adventist parents recognize this superiority but care more about other facets of education that non-Adventist schools offer (sports programs, internships, exchange programs, etc.), and enroll their students elsewhere accordingly. And third, it may be that many Adventist parents realize that Adventist schools are academically superior to public schools . . . and it doesn't impress them very much. Which leads to:

2. Academics may still need to be listed as a quality concern in spite of the positive CognitiveGenesis results *because we may be aiming too low.*

In the minds of many, public education in the United States is a questionable benchmark for Adventist education to pursue. Case in point: Have you noticed that the past several presidential election cycles have regularly put substantial focus on improving America's public schools? The reason for it is no secret. Public schools are facing great challenges with the quality of their academic program! So do we want to exceed public schools academically? Emphatically, yes. But we must not merely exceed them—*we must put considerable academic daylight between them and us.*

Think of it like this: Few of you would be impressed if I told you that I can beat five-foot-three TV reporter Barbara Walters in a game of basketball. But if I claimed that I can and have beaten multitime NBA champion Kobe Bryant every year for the past 10 years, you just might stop and take notice.[3] In the same way, it is possible that a positive CognitiveGenesis report will bring us both good news and bad. The good news: We are academically superior to public schools. The bad news: Not by enough.

Again, all of this is speculative. As of this writing the CognitiveGenesis report has not yet finished. It may yet turn out that academics are not a quality concern in our schools. But one thing is in my opinion definitely not speculative. Too many Adventists do not *perceive* our schools as academically adequate. Again, witness the stunning number of our high school graduates who choose to go to non-Adventist universities, many of them because of their perception that our colleges and universities are academically inferior. We can question these students' values or whether they possibly place prestige above spiritual enrichment. But the perception of questionable academic quality is currently real and will continue to affect our enrollment unless we actively and decisively counteract it with strong information to the contrary.

## Quality Concern 5:
## Ignorance of Prophetic Counsel

Ellen White wrote a great deal about Adventist education. Yet teachers and laypeople alike often neglect her counsel—at times totally. While it's true that she never provided a "one size fits all" model for all Adventist schools to follow, she most certainly did offer a number of principles that, if followed, would give many of our schools a decided boost in both mission effectiveness and, I believe, enrollment. Yet her primary work in this regard—the book *Education*—remains a literary backwater to far too many of those involved in Adventist education.

For instance, we almost universally ignore her inspired counsels on student labor. True, we no longer live in an agricultural society in which students can learn work habits on the school farm as easily as they did 100 years ago. However, the solution is most certainly not to make student labor optional. In fact, in today's world in which couch potato-ism flourishes as never before, a great portion of our students come to our schools with perhaps the worst collective work ethic seen in recent history. I don't think I'm being overly dramatic here. I've known of high school students who genuinely don't know how to use a broom or how to turn on a vacuum cleaner—not because they're idiots, but because they've never done it before. Keeping one's room clean at boarding academy, being on time to class, finishing homework on time, and many other things, are all becoming increasingly lost arts among too many of our students.

And in the face of all this, many of our academies, for instance, respond by . . . making student labor optional? Let us be crystal clear: Ellen White's concern that students work with the soil was not only about the soil, but about the student. An idle mind is still the devil's workshop, and for us to allow students to choose whether or not they will have a job or not is ludicrous. So what if we can no longer make a school farm viable? What industry *can* we operate successfully that will enable our students to learn proper work habits and become productive church members and members of society?

We also pay little attention to a number of other topics that she argues for forcibly. Our schools cafeterias regularly thwart out health message. The diet they offer is often too short on fresh fruits, nuts, and fresh vegetables and too long on fat, salt, and sugar. I am not being a fanatic here— I like dessert in moderation as much as the next person (I tend to agree with my grandmother, who says that the fruit on the tree of life will actually be chocolate). But in, say, an elementary or high school environment, in which childhood obesity rates in the U.S. are approaching *one third* of the youth population and early-onset diabetes has grown by leaps and bounds, why on God's green earth would any school—especially an Adventist one!—offer anything less than the highest quality fuel for its students' bodies? Not only would students enjoy better physical health, but truancy rates, missed assignments, and inattentiveness would also all decrease accordingly, and they would form other healthy habits, as well.

Until we attend to such counsel in these areas and others (such as dress, entertainment, and social conduct addressed earlier), many concerned Adventists—including those with ample financial resources to pay tuition in full—will continue to refuse to enroll their students in our schools.

## Quality Concern 6:
## Inroads of Postmodern Thought

This concern has a close relationship to concern 2 regarding a lack of passion for things uniquely Adventist, and of course we have already discussed it at length in chapter 6. So I'll now make some specific applications to Adventist campus and classroom life.

It would be wonderful to be able to say that postmodernism—which rules Hollywood and nearly all of the public education system, especially at the postsecondary level—has not touched Adventist campuses or classrooms. But that would be false. They most certainly have been affected, and at times in painful ways.

For example, most of our students (and many of our staff members) have spent a great deal of time watching a lot of television. We find some great shows on TV, shows that can teach our kids some wonderful things. But unfortunately, television is also one of the prime mediums for postmodern thought and secularism. And if parents aren't careful what their kids watch, the influence of TV too often means that students bring with them to class a mind-set that says this: Violence, open sexuality, gross immorality, etc., are not only *not* automatically evil, but are actually subjects for one's personal entertainment. (Pop music and many darker video games, which so often glorify the aforementioned sins, are also rampant among Adventist students, contributing further to moral relativism.)

So how does this affect Adventist education? Simply put, when a postmodern-influenced student goes to class and comes up against Adventist claims of absolute truth, such as "Jesus is the only path to eternal life" or "the Sabbath occurs only from Friday sundown to Saturday sundown and can be truly kept only during those hours," such a young person pushes back forcibly. And if we don't respond to that reaction appropriately (through open, relational dialogue and consistently enforced boundaries), campus life soon emulates the very things the students have seen or heard repeatedly on TV or the radio or through other mediums. The danger is thus twofold: (1) students infected with postmodern principles may come to our schools predisposed to reject Adventist values personally, and (2) when unregulated or if present in sufficient numbers, they may come to dominate the campus "flavor" and activities on a corporate level. If the latter happens, many Adventist parents keep shopping for another school.

Lest you think I'm a puritan on steroids, I'd challenge you to call up some of our Adventist chaplains or Bible teachers at our academies or colleges/universities. Most will tell you story after story of outrageous claims made by Adventist students with regard to proper conduct socially, sexually, etc., that should help remove doubts as to the inroads of postmodern/secular thinking in our students—much of which came to them through the popular media.

And what about staff influenced by postmodern thinking and secularism? While in my experience less prolific than among the students, such teachers have nonetheless made their homes in Adventist classrooms more than many would like to admit.

(An interesting corollary to this is the increasing number of non-Adventist teachers in the world church. At the October 14, 2005, General Conference Annual Council, the report of the Commission on Higher Education showed that in 1990 non-Adventist faculty the world over amounted to just 4 percent of the total teaching staff. However, by the year 2000 the number had risen to 16 percent, and by 2010 it is projected to be at least 28 percent.[4] While not always the case, it is possible and perhaps likely that such non-Adventist staff will be more open to postmodern thought and certainly less committed to Adventist-specific values.)

Part of the phenomenon of postmodern-influenced staff is, while not excusable, somewhat explainable. For instance, among college professors, the old mantra "publish or perish" still holds true. Colleges understandably want the wider world to perceive their faculty as competent and creative—and thus attractive to prospective students and financial donors. Fine. But for many professors, having the name of an Adventist institution of higher learning tacked on to the end of their byline makes professional relationships harder, not easier (it's that "weird" factor again that we talked about in chapter 1). And in their rush to find acceptance outside of the church, the temptation to embrace the spirit of this age (moral relativism) can be very strong indeed, especially if that can lead to greater prestige and professional advancement.

But again, while this is an explanation, it is neither a complete one nor even an acceptable excuse. I see the facts as these: While Adventism has great room for debate about various topics, we cannot say the same about the essential core that has always comprised Adventism. For instance, the Bible ought always to be considered essential, authoritative, and necessary for healthy spiritual life; Christ as personal Friend and Savior ought to be expected and required for all teachers; faith integrity—that is, that our faith is meant to be actually lived out consistently and in relationship with others—ought to be seen as indispensable; the nearness of Christ's coming ought always to profoundly influence our personal and corporate decisions; the Sabbath ought always to be honored and be intentionally and joyfully observed; prophecy, whether in the Bible or in the ministry of Ellen White, ought always to be taken seriously, regardless of whether we all agree on the specific interpretation of this passage or that. It is a relatively small core! But many of our schools and their teachers often ignore even this low threshold. I cannot count the times that I've visited with teachers at various levels—college, high school, or elementary—and probed about their passion or even mere belief in this brief but vital core and been profoundly disappointed. These things are essential to our identity as Adventists, yet we too often treat them as though they're quaint relics from our theological redneck past.

Let me quickly add that I've met an even greater number of staff and teachers that *are* dedicated to central Adventist ideals. They believe in the core deeply, teach it passionately, and live it out in their own lives. For this majority I praise the Lord! But in my opinion it is a slim majority. And to prove the point, let me ask the teachers reading this book: Can you name the people on the staff of your school right now who are passionately, compassionately, and openly *Adventist?* On the other hand, can you name the staff members for whom Adventism generates no passion (though they may profess Christ), individuals who either privately or publicly have no love for their church other than that it provides them with a salary and a venue to express their own ideas? My guess is that if your experience is like mine, you can quickly cite people in both categories.

Many have wondered why the Adventist Church continues to pay the teachers in the second category just described. Increasingly, many Adventists are deciding not to. They demonstrate that by no longer sending their own children to be taught by them. And until the administration and boards of our schools are willing to lovingly hold such staff accountable, this negative trend will continue. We must preserve freedom of inquiry, but never at the expense of exchanging the Adventist core for a shadowy image of its former self.

## Quality Concern 7:
## Poor Physical Plant Condition

I almost hesitate to mention this one, because the ability to solve it lies at times outside of a given school. But I need to mention it nonetheless, as it does affect parents' decisions as to whether or not to enroll their child(ren) in our schools.

My friend Rob Smith, who works as the assistant secretary of education for the Potomac Conference, recently made an excellent observation. As part of his work Rob travels extensively and visits a lot of schools. "It's amazing to see the condition of [the physical plant in] many of our schools," he said. "I went to elementary school in the 1970s, and when I walk into many of our elementary schools today, it's as if nothing has changed since then!"

Unfortunately, he's right. The 1950s, 1960s, and 1970s boomed with new construction in the Adventist Church (and many other denominations, for that matter—again, wider societal trends at work), and new churches and new schools multiplied like proverbial rabbits. As the prosperous years continued, we were able to update our buildings as needed . . . until the boom stopped. And unfortunately, hundreds of our schools' physical plants across the country today need repair, renovation, or even demolition. (A standing joke at one of the church schools I served with was that the best thing that could happen to our physical plant was a good fire. But then again, that probably wouldn't have worked: The building was too waterlogged to burn.)

Naturally, this has an effect on enrollment for some parents, particular the handful of non-Adventist parents who might consider sending their children to our schools. What would you think if you walked into a school and the first thing you noticed was the smell of mildew? What if the classrooms looked extraordinarily well appointed—for 1968? What if water damage discolored most of the ceiling tiles, or if the bathrooms had leaky and ancient fixtures, or if the playground equipment resembled leftovers from a government tetanus infliction test site? That's right: You'd take your kids elsewhere, or at the very least commit only tentatively to having your kids at that school over the long haul.

Again, I must point out that many schools are stuck with their aging physical plants. Most principals can't wave a magic wand and receive $250,000 to fix the worst of their physical plant problems. Our schools in this regard are thus at times victims of the many reasons for Adventist educational decline that I've spent the previous chapters outlining. But regardless of whose fault it is, decrepit physical plants are a real problem in our schools, and represent a quality concern that must—and I believe can—be addressed if our educational institutions are to move forward into health.

---

[1] George Knight, *Myths in Adventism* (Hagerstown, Md.: Review and Herald Pub. Assn., 1985), pp. 47-51.

[2] Follow the study's progress and results at www.cognitivegenesis.org.

[3] I can't, and I haven't. But you'd still be impressed, wouldn't you?

[4] R. Bruinsma, "The Quest for Integrity," p. 23.

PART THREE:

# RECIPE FOR DESTRUCTION

# CHAPTER 8

# How to Kill
# Adventist Education

We can sum up the way to kill Adventist education in five words. While we rarely voice them, they are often implemented. Some of us don't like these five words, and I cannot recall a single school principal or board or teacher who has ever publicly professed their allegiance to them. But they are too often a reality, nonetheless, for these five words appear to promise safety—and for those in denominational employ, they even appear to guarantee job security. The five words that describe how to eradicate Adventist education are:

## Keep doing what we're doing.

Is this plan being successfully implemented in your school?

To state the obvious, *we've got to do something different than what we're currently doing if our particular school is tanking. New methods—and perhaps some old yet good methods that we have left behind—must be discovered and implemented. New life can come to our schools. But if transformation is to happen, we must change course. We must start afresh and follow a new path.*

Which brings us to part four.

# PART FOUR:
## SOME POSSIBLE SOLUTIONS TO THE CRISIS

# CHAPTER 9

# How to Give Adventist
# Education a Fighting Chance

Whew! At last we can get to some solutions. What will it take to move Adventist education to a place at which it is not merely surviving, but thriving?

A quick perusal of the causes of Adventist education's demise suggests that two broad areas especially need attention: the local church and the local school. This leads me to point out that when it comes to turning our schools around, there is both good news and bad news.

## The Good News First

The good news is that experience has shown that schools that implement the steps I'll describe in the coming pages can indeed turn back from the brink of destruction into genuine, vibrant health. To prove the point, I will sprinkle the remaining chapters with examples from two boarding academies—Mount Vernon Academy in Ohio and Shenandoah Valley Academy in Virginia—to illustrate what can happen when we apply the right principles in the right way. Let's take a brief look at each school.

Mount Vernon Academy (MVA) has deep roots in the Adventist Church, tracing its heritage all the way back to 1885, when the denomination purchased its site with seed moneys totaling $10,000 (a handsome sum at the time and an indication of the passion that accompanied MVA's genesis). For the next 75 years MVA grew from mere dream to an overflowing reality, ultimately reaching a student body of more than 320 students in the 1960s.

But in the 1970s that enrollment began a gradual but steady decline. By the late 1990s student count had dropped so badly that for several years running the Ohio Conference and MVA board strongly considered recommending the closure of MVA. In the spring of 2000 closing enrollment was a stark 78 students (and only seven of those were freshmen!)—hardly enough to maintain a quality educational environment, much less move confidently forward into the future.

Then in 2001 the academy began to undergo a radical transformation. Under the leadership of a new principal, Dale Twomley, the campus changed drastically in nearly every area: academics, physical plant, school policy, behavioral guidelines, and of course spirituality. And what was the result? The very next school year, enrollment shot up to 122 students. The following year's student count was in the 140s, and by the 2006-2007 school year, opening enrollment reached 168—*more than twice the number of students a mere six years before.* True, it is still down from the level of the 1960s. But today MVA is nonetheless a thriving school with high-quality spirituality and academics, a renewed physical plant, and a great deal of enthusiasm among staff and students alike. (And yes: they're financially solvent.) Not bad for an institution that less than a decade ago was on the verge of closing.[1]

And how did this come about? Certainly it involved many factors. But on the whole, *MVA transformed itself by implementing the change process described in the pages ahead.*

Shenandoah Valley Academy (SVA) is another of our schools with a rich history. Begun in 1908 on land donated by a bed-bound and dying Charles Zirkle, SVA went on to become another educational powerhouse in the North American Division. Such was its reputation in fact for outstanding academics and music that it became known to some as "The Jewel of the Eastern Seaboard." Small wonder that SVA's enrollment topped 320 students even as late as the 1980s.

But by the 1990s it had begun a long but steady slide. By 2004 SVA had lost approximately 10 students every year for the previous 11 years. Then, at the opening of the 2006-2007 school year, enrollment dropped off a cliff. Though the board had budgeted for 205 students, only 135 actually registered. It represented an immediate operational loss of more than $700,000, accompanied by a massive drop in campus morale.

Faced with the single largest loss in the history of SVA and possible closure, the Potomac Conference and SVA board moved swiftly. Dale Twomley (there's that guy, again) assumed the principalship and immediately began to overhaul the school. As with Mount Vernon Academy, SVA left no stone unturned in its quest to revitalize itself. It scrutinized, streamlined, and improved everything from staffing to finances to curriculum to dorm life and beyond.

The results were immediate and dramatic. The graduating class of 2006-2007 (the year in which enrollment dropped so precipitously) was more than 60 students strong, meaning that nearly half the school would be exiting that spring. But even with this significant loss, enrollment in the 2007-2008 school year was more than 170 students! In what must rank as some kind of record in the history of secondary education in the NAD, it meant that SVA—a mere one year after its catastrophic drop in enrollment—attracted *more than 100 brand-new enrollees.* (Note that more than 40 of those were previously attending public school.) The following year only continued this success, with SVA averaging nearly 220 students for the 2008-2009 school year (and again, many of the new students had previously been attending public school.) Additionally, confidence in the "new" SVA, as it's been called, has grown such that it received more than $3 million in the next three years from alumni and other donors to go toward its physical plant renovation projects. It gave the campus two completely re-modeled dormitories as well as a remodeled student center and ad building welcome area. As I write this, the school is building new ball fields, and the spirit on campus is highly spiritual and very energetic. Once again SVA is a place to which parents delight to send their kids.

As with MVA's turnaround, many factors were in play. But on the whole, *Shenandoah Valley Academy transformed itself through implementing the change process outlined in the pages ahead.*

Now, some of you may be tempted to say that the actual lesson MVA and SVA teach us is "If your school is in trouble, hire Dale Twomley." And indeed, in my opinion, he is one of the most skilled leaders and administrators in the North American Division. But he would also be the first to tell you that it does-n't take him to turn a school around. Instead, *it requires principles, rightly applied, by leaders who refuse to settle for business as usual—leaders who regard their calling from God so seriously that they will not rest until their school fully glorifies God.* We will look at the principles and how to apply them to your school in the pages ahead.

## The Choice of These Two Schools

In spite of the dramatic nature of the MVA and SVA transformations, some may still question the validity of using their stories to inform other educational situations. After all, both schools are boarding academies and thus are becoming increasingly rare entities in the NAD. Also, a number of elementary schools have had equally dramatic turnarounds. Why not cite them as examples instead?

Let me hasten to say that the change process I'll outline in the coming pages is a synthesis of lessons indeed exemplified in MVA and SVA. But I have also gleaned insights from a host of other schools and educational leaders across the North American Division. And my experience in gathering information for this book leads me to conclude that, while other turnarounds have occurred, these two schools are especially helpful examples of how transformation can occur in nearly any school—and that, for at least two reasons.

The first reason is simple: The MVA and SVA stories are fresh. They didn't happen 50 or even 15 years ago, but within the past decade. Thus they provide up-to-date case studies in a rapidly changing world that can help other schools in the same historical milieu.

But second (and I think more compellingly), *nothing compares with the pressure-cooker, complex environment of a boarding academy*. No, other school types are not cakewalks. But the boarding academy beast has something particularly intense about it.

For instance, consider the student side of the boarding academy equation. The students (as with all high schools) necessarily run the gamut from extraordinarily immature to very mature young adults—a volatile and challenging brew for any teacher/staff member to deal with. But because parents send their kids to a boarding academy not merely to take some classes but to actually live there, its campus standards—and the performance standards of their teachers and staff—must be sky-high. Faults that some might excuse on a day school campus are often unacceptable on a boarding school campus, simply because parents of boarding academy students know they won't be present to clean up whatever mess has resulted. Thus a boarding school campus has relatively little margin for error, and students must be extraordinarily well cared for or else the school will close.

Moreover, in addition to the normal teaching load that any Adventist high school expects its teachers to carry, boarding academy faculty also have to assume heavy supervision duties after hours and nearly every weekend. Unlike a day academy, students are nearly always present on campus during the school year. Add to the boarding academy teacher's load some class and/or club sponsorships, the requisite field trips (which rarely enjoy the parental support that day academy field trips often do), and the fact that teachers and staff essentially live with their students, and it's no mystery why many boarding academy teachers and staff are a very special breed of human being. They are the Green Berets of Adventist education, and while it requires an extraordinary amount of dedication to be an effective Adventist teacher anywhere, it is perhaps no more so demanded than at a boarding academy.

So here's the point: boarding academy faculty, staff, and students work and live together under some of the most extreme conditions that North American Adventism can offer—and if the solutions I'll be sharing for turning around a declining school can work there, chances are good that they'll function elsewhere as well. Good news!

## However . . .

Unfortunately, there is some bad news, too. Of the six causes of Adventist educational demise given in part two of this book, at least three of them occur almost exclusively in the local church, not the school—which leads to an uncomfortable conclusion: It is entirely possible that we must do much of the turnaround work in the local church/local supporting constituency rather than the local school itself. This also means—and here's the bad news—*that a school could fully implement the solutions suggested in the coming pages . . . and still close its doors if it's saddled with an overly unhealthy local church or supporting constituency.*

I wish I could say differently, but I can't. Constituencies and schools often engage in complex dances with one another that make it difficult for one to go in a new direction without the other. So the heavier partner often wins. If you begin to turn around an Adventist elementary school, for instance, but have a local pastor or two determined to cut off support for it, success is going to be hard to come by no matter how high the quality of the school may be.

Add to this the fact that the majority of the rest of this book will deal with the local school and not its constituency,[2] and you may wonder why you should bother reading the solutions I propose!

I hate suspense. Here's why you should not only keep reading about, but start implementing as soon as possible, the proposed solutions that lie ahead.

1. *Trying to turn around an Adventist school is almost always the right thing to do.* True, some schools are too far gone to save. They need euthanizing, mourning, and then burying. But many, many, many Adventist schools can be resurrected.

And in those situations in which they should be, trying to return them to health is a God-given duty that demands our best energies, most impassioned efforts, and lavish donations of time, money, and prayer. The salvation of countless students may depend on it. The future success of the Adventist Church may rest on it. And thus, in nearly every case, resurrecting a school is simply the right thing to do regardless of whether or not we have the assurance that our local constituency will support us.

2. *Local constituencies often become more supportive of schools making serious efforts to transform themselves.* A hostile constituency can change for the better when they see their local school seriously attempting to alter the way it functions (and in chapter 10 I'll give some specific suggestions for helping the various levels of your supporting constituency become more enthusiastic for transforming your school).

3. *If you don't try to turn your school around, you guarantee that it won't turn around!* It is true that an unsupportive local church or constituency can be a major obstacle to transitioning your school back to health. But if you don't forge ahead anyway, you virtually guarantee that the school will stay in decline or perhaps even die. We've got to remember that God is still alive, and that He's still in the business of miraculous transformations. Why not do your part and begin to transform your school, all the while praying that He will change hearts and minds in its constituency so that they can make the transformation lasting and complete?

## Getting Ready: The Need to Start Locally

The number one reason for the decline in Adventist education has to do with our division-wide lack of a sense of our unique Adventist selves. We have too often lost our taste for living in uniquely Adventist ways, and we thus are murky on our Adventist identity.

From that reasoning we might find ourselves tempted to think that the implementation of any solution to our problems might start at the division level. But I don't think that is the case. For while ultimately we do have to address our ignorance/apathy concerning Adventism's special calling at a division-wide level (as well as some pivotal administrative issues—see chapter 19), we nonetheless must start fixing our problem right here at home first.

A couple reasons demand this. First, the problems in many of our local schools are acute. As a result, we may not have the luxury of waiting for a divi-sion-wide renewed appreciation of Adventism, for instance, to kick in and even-tually affect our particular school. Second, the local school's interface with parents is, well, local. A division-wide campaign for education renewal, while es-sential and overdue, is not going to help entice local parents right off the bat. That must come from one place most forcibly and most effectively: your local school/academy/college/university. Thus we'll begin at home with your local institution, and then later on we'll move to potential division-wide solutions.

## An Eight-Step Strategy, Plus One

The suggestions that I'm going to make to you in the remaining pages will certainly not apply equally to every Adventist school. Local context counts for a lot and will directly influence our ability to implement any suggestions, no matter how good they may otherwise be. However, I also believe that the strat-egy I'm going to outline is simple and effective enough to use in a majority of the situations in which one of our schools finds itself floundering. Tweak it/alter it/add to it as necessary for your local situation.

We must take at least eight key steps plus one "always step" in order to have the greatest possibility of returning a school in poor health to a thriving state. The steps are as follows:

1. Ask and answer the right questions.
2. Become a school of prayer.
3. Find the right local leader.
4. Discover the true state of your school.
5. Master the fundamentals of Adventist education.
6. Relentlessly eliminate weaknesses or make them irrelevant.
7. Get the good word out/enlist widespread support.
8. Embed the positive changes in the culture of the school.

## And finally, the "always step": Pursue transformational money.

That's the plan. We'll unpack it, step by step, in the chapters ahead.

---

[1] For a good synopsis of MVA's history and turnaround, see the Columbia Union *Visitor*, March 2007, pp. 8–11.

[2] There are a number of specific and helpful things that one can do to encourage unsup-portive local churches and constituencies to become advocates for Adventist education. Space constraints prohibit me from covering them in this book.

# CHAPTER 10

# Step 1:
# Ask and Answer
# the Right Questions

One of the ironic truths about Adventist educational demise is that it's been a long time in the making. To my knowledge, none of our schools that have shut down or faced closure were unaware that they had problems for years in advance. For instance, SVA had a 15-year period of decline, while MVA had a nearly 30-year one. The point is simple: The specter of closure made itself obvious through the simple extrapolation of long-term enrollment trends.

But seeing future failure and choosing to take whatever action necessary to stave it off are two different things. And instead of meeting the problems head-on and finding solutions to them, we too often have chosen any number of alternate—and ineffective—routes.

For instance, when faced with yet another drop in enrollment, instead of finding out why and fixing the problem, many have waxed nostalgic and reminisced about the "good old days" (almost as though that were a solution in itself). Others have immersed themselves in dealing with the financial shortfalls. "What we need is more money!" they say, when the truth is that money is almost always a *secondary* indicator. It is a symptom of the problem, not the problem itself! So while our ledgers should be in order, we must stop imagining that the solution to our big problem—low student count because of low educational quality or other issues—will get solved by a finance committee.

Instead of dodging the issues that will kill our schools, here are the hard questions that we must ask and answer correctly before we should ever make any attempt at a return to school health.

*1. Am I willing to admit my part in this problem?* If you've been a teacher, board member, principal, or other educational leader in a declining school for three years or more, *the problems of that school are in some measure yours.* You can no longer lay blame on previous administrations and "how incompetent" they were and thus dodge responsibility yourself. *Take the blame yourself, for only then can you have a chance at fixing the problem.* Own it and fix it—but you can't do the latter unless you first do the former.

*2. Do I have a compelling vision for the future of my school?* Ah, crucial stuff here! There is no substitute for a well-defined and thoroughly inspiring picture of what your school can become if God blesses while people work smart and hard.

Why is such a vision so crucial? Because leaders who seek to change an educational institution have little with which to motivate the possible supporters of that transformation unless they can cogently tell the story of "what can be" in their school. Constituents need to see the sweetness of a possible future before they'll fully engage in escaping the vinegar of the present! And no, this is not an exercise in dreaming up impossible goals ("We believe our K-12 program will become the sole feeder school for Harvard" and similar thoughts are fantasies, not visions). It is instead—and follow me closely here—a matter of *listening to the voice of God, both currently and via the history of the school.*

A good example is what happened at SVA. When Dale Twomley arrived at the academy, the mood was understandably grim. Enrollment had plummeted, staff cuts had been made, and the future was at best uncertain. But into that depressing brew came a fresh vision of the future based on two things. First, Twomley made it clear that from his perspective he was on the grounds at all "because God has called us [my wife and me] to be here." That's part of listening to the voice of God in the present, and this in itself was helpful to the SVA staff.* But Twomley also began to articulate clearly what SVA had been in the past, and that through God's blessing and hard work it could regain and even exceed those old glories. Staff meetings became venues to recount memories of previous outstanding staff members as well as unique and gifted former students, special relationships, and successes. And Twomley followed up those recollections with some version of "God's not done with Shenandoah yet. It can rise again! God and we together can turn this place around to where it excels spiritually, academically, musically, whatever, as it has before!" The results soon spoke for themselves, particularly when it involved alumni. (Remember, a large portion of the $3 million SVA received for capital improvements came from them. They remembered SVA's glory days and wanted to see them return.)

At MVA the story was much the same. In the process of kicking off the turnaround, Mount Vernon revisited names, events, and successes from its golden age. As the school recalled grand old staff members, it reminded listeners just how much God had blessed the school in the past. Twomley made it clear: "No more talk *ever* about closing this school. God and we are going to return MVA to its former state and beyond." And again the results speak for themselves. Staff, students, parents, and alumni bought into the vision, eventually providing waves of momentum that revealed themselves in donations of time, money, and materials for transforming the campus.

So what about you? Do you have a compelling vision of the future for your school? Dispense with the very uncompelling one of "Boy, I hope we survive this next year!" and replace it with private time with God and the history (literally, "His story") of your school and of Adventist education in general. (A reread of Ellen White's book *Education* may be extraordinarily helpful as well—it is a wonderfully visionary book.) Pray and plan, asking God to show you what He wants your school to look like in the future. Talk with others to whom God may also be speaking. Formulate the vision so that it's clear in your mind. Then present it to your constituents, whoever and wherever they may be, *and never stop proclaiming it.* That vision is your goal, your rudder, your inducement to colaborers in transformation. Treat it as the gold it is, and avoid moving forward in the change process until this vision is clear. Without it you—and your school—will almost certainly fail to thrive.

*3. Am I willing to do* anything *that's moral and ethical to see my school return to health?* If the answer is no, then you may want to consider resigning whatever your position is in your particular educational institution.

I am completely serious about this. And I'm not trying to be cruel or harsh, but rather am simply highlighting the simple facts: *If you want your school to thrive again, it will cost you.* The devil hates God and His schools, and if you think the devil—or tradition or inertia or whatever—will roll over and play dead just because you've decided to improve your school, the litany of now-*deceased* Adventist schools says otherwise. The road to health is definitely passable, but it will require a great deal from those who wish to traverse it successfully.

So be honest: Do you *really* want your school to thrive? Do you *really* want to stop doing school the way you've been doing it and start doing it the right way regardless of the cost? Are you personally/as a board/as a principal/as a church administrator willing to pay the price to see vibrancy return, even if that means (for instance) firing long-term but troublesome staff, stopping or dramatically altering longstanding but damaging school traditions, or taking calculated but nonetheless dangerous risks—and in the process having some people become foot-stomping mad at you?

If the answer is a no or a maybe, then you may want to make sure that your wardrobe includes something black—a school funeral may be looming soon on the horizon.

But if your answer is a solid yes, praise the Lord! You're on the right track. After all, it's no coincidence that the schools that have returned to health after grave illness are those who finally came to the place where things were so bad that school leadership became desperate and thus quite willing at last to make changes that often should have taken place years earlier. But why not give it all you've got now? God's kids need Adventist education! There are few more noble causes to which you could dedicate your life to. *Pay the price for the restoration of your school!* The kingdom of heaven will be a bigger and better place if you do.

4. *Are there enough of the right people in the right places to accomplish what our school needs?* Making the kind of changes required to move a school back into health goes much more smoothly if there exists widespread support among staff, faculty (particularly the school administrator), and board members (and for conference or union institutions, conference or union board members). As I referred to in chapter 9, if you do not have sufficient support at these levels, change will be all the more difficult and at times impossible.

But what if you're the lone ranger at your school? For instance, what if you're a school principal or board member and see legitimate and potentially deadly signs of decline, yet few others in leadership share your concerns? In this situation you could explore several possible avenues to gather support.

First, pray. God can pull strings that you haven't thought of. So pray, and don't stop till something changes (and then keep praying anyway—you'll need it).

Second, become a polite but persistent burr under the appropriate people's saddles. For instance, continue politely but firmly to bring up signs of decline to (for instance) the board, and push for recognition of the developing or worsening problem. It may not win you friends, but then again, this is not a popularity contest. Always be loving, always be honest, and you'll be able to sleep well at night even if your local board does not receive your messages well.

Third, those of you who are principals, presidents, board chairs, etc. (that is, those of you in senior leadership positions) may want to consider "creating a crisis" that will direct attention to the reality of your school's decline. I'm not joking. Remember, *one of the primary jobs of leadership is to define reality*. If the reality in your school is "We're dying," then you've got to get that message through your leaders' heads—and a crisis can be a good way to do it. Here's a couple of ways to instigate such a situation.

Get a chart illustrating in big, bold graphics the decline over the past 10, 20, or 30 years of your school's enrollment. Illustrate the problem clearly and honestly, making those prone to engage in "happy talk" instead of positive action as uncomfortable as possible.

Do the same with finances. Sad to say, but some of our institutions get off center only when their pocketbook is in jeopardy. So show how much danger it's in. Chart the ever-increasing subsidy your school has required from your constituents. Show how short on cash the school is. Make dire (and true, of course) predictions of what will happen if nothing changes and soon.

Give parents proper access to your board. Many boards are isolated from the very people who pay the bills—mom and dad. If the latter are disgruntled (and potentially considering pulling their kids from your school because of potentially changeable—but currently unchanging—issues at your school), hear their concerns out privately and, when appropriate, let them present them openly to the board. This can be particularly effective with the boards of secondary or postsecondary schools, as those boards tend to be the most insulated from parental views (often because of the fact that many of those types of boards consist of people who live out of the school's home area).

(This suggestion is getting a little ahead of ourselves, but I'll mention it briefly here and expand on it more in chapter 13.) Another way to call attention to your school's crisis is to bring in a consultant or advisory team that you trust. Have them evaluate your school. Let them present to your board and faculty the problems as they see them. Such an approach may help your leadership to recognize the need for new approaches far more quickly than if just you made such suggestions. Remember, an "expert," as they say, is anyone who lives more than 100 miles away, and if you call in such people who pronounce dire consequences for your school unless A, B, and C change and soon, it just might carry the day and create a willingness to move forward.

In some instances you need to take full advantage of a crisis that arises without your generating it. Classic case: As I mentioned earlier, by 2004 SVA had lost approximately 10 students each year for the previous 11 years. One would think that fact would have been cause for great alarm. Yet no efforts to stem the tide were successful until 2006, when student enrollment fell below the previous year by nearly six times the "normal" amount. Instant crisis! And very helpful, too, as it finally initiated the systemic changes needed to return the school to vibrancy. Don't let such opportunities pass you by! Grab them, trumpet reality, and use the urgency generated to institute the necessary adjustments or modifications.

However you go about it, do your best to make sure that you have a sufficiently powerful guiding coalition to accomplish successfully what your school needs.

A final note on this point: One possible exception to the above advice occurs when (1) the school is truly teetering on the edge of immediate closure; (2) there is no sign of great interest in fixing the problem; and (3) the school is worth saving. Then every leader, regardless of the support they have, must do their level best to save the school through all means ethical and moral. There is something to be said for being able to stand before God with a clear conscience, knowing that you did what you could even though you stood alone. And who knows but that God may be waiting for someone to take such a position so that He may pour out His power and bring about the necessary backing from others?

So ask and answer the right questions. When you've got the right answers, you're ready for step 2.

---

* There are generally only two kinds of leaders that come on board at schools that just lost a third of their enrollment: people called of God, and fools. The staff was inspired and relieved to learn that Twomley belonged to the former category rather than the latter.

# CHAPTER 11

# Step 2:
# Become a School of Prayer

I don't want to spend a lot of time on this one. Not because it's not important, but because it's the most important of any of the action-oriented steps in the eight-step process. If I concentrate too much time on it, you might be tempted to lose focus. So here's my take on turning your school into a school of prayer.

*1. Just do it—pray, that is.* We do not need another seminar on prayer how-to's—we must pray. Nor do we need to convene another meeting in which we vote that prayer is a good thing, or to read another book on how important it is to share our hearts with God. We just must actually pray! This is not rocket science! Let us stop the posturing, admit our deep and constant need of God, and then act as if we believe it. That is, let us truly stop what we're doing regularly and begin to really pray.

You can do all the rest of these eight steps, yet without the prayer step you'll fail. Or at best, you'll succeed at the wrong things. Adventist educational decline is indeed often a matter of run-of-the-mill quality issues. But Adventist schools are to be *spiritual* organisms—that is, engendered, created, and sustained by the Holy Spirit. When you skip prayer, you bypass the Holy Spirit's day-to-day input on what move to make now, what's the next top priority issue, etc. Let the Spirit lead. And that can be done only when we pray regularly.

*2. Pray as a staff and student body daily.* Make it more than the simple (though necessary) prayers said at the starting or ending of the school day. Rather, have a special time—perhaps 15-20 minutes—in the middle of your day, during which your entire school body (staff, teachers, students, whomever) all pause and pray.

Both MVA and SVA did it to great effect via something called Faculty Families. The schools asked all available staff to be heads of these units, which consisted of themselves plus 6-12 students. Each day (usually late morning or midday) all classes and appointments would cease so that the head of the Faculty Families could meet with their students. The sessions would share prayer requests, air concerns and praises, and of course, pray. Such meetings have proved to be very helpful in bathing the respective campuses in a spirit of prayer and attentiveness to God.

Also consider setting aside meaningful time for your staff meetings and board meetings to engage in prayer. If you have one, ask your Home and School Association to pray regularly for the school. Plead with God for revival and renewal, as well as for the prayer requests that the students or staff may bring up. Again, this is letting the Spirit return to the driver's seat of your school. He may not have sat there for a while, but we can be assured that He most certainly needs to occupy that position now if your change efforts are to be successful and more than cosmetic.

3. *Engage your whole constituency in prayer for your school.* All Adventist schools have broader constituencies, whether they be a local church or churches or a conference or union. Involve them in prayer for your school. Share your needs with them specifically and enlist their prayer support—preferably in writing.* The Shenandoah Valley Academy campus church has hundreds of active members who have no family connection with (i.e., no enrolled students at) SVA. But in 2004 a program called ROK (Reach Our Kids) began, and quickly became the single largest ministry that the church had (it is still running strong today). Of the many activities ROK initiated, one of the best had to do with prayer. More than 100 members received specific names of students that they then began to pray for. (And though we may not know for sure till heaven, it is entirely possible that one of the major factors in finally bringing about the resurgence of spiritual life on the SVA campus was the fact that every day for years dozens and dozens of people prayed for students specifically and the school in general.)

God is waiting. Become a school of prayer!

---

* Be honest: How many times have you forgotten to pray for someone after they asked, "Would you pray for me?" and you said yes? Increase your effectiveness in enlisting prayer support for your school by giving potential pray-ers requests in writing, preferably gently requiring them to return something to you indicating their intentions to pray for you.

# CHAPTER 12

# Step 3:
# Find the Right Local Leader

This one is a bit ticklish, but is absolutely crucial to your school's success. After the leadership of the Holy Spirit, your school's next-greatest need is the right human leader to guide the charge back to health. Every story in the Bible in which renewal occurs has near its heart a called and qualified individual. And today we need Joshuas, Gideons, Davids, and Pauls just as urgently as they were needed long ago, to see God's work through to fruition.

At both Mount Vernon Academy and Shenandoah Valley Academy Dale Twomley proved to be the leader required. God was able to utilize his skills and giftedness to great effect. But again, he is not the key to every school's transformation. Rather, qualified and competent leadership—regardless of who's wielding it—can yield tremendous results for troubled institutions.

The ticklish part is, of course, that the administrators you currently have at your school may or may not be those transformational individuals—and if not (forgive me for my bluntness here), they need to be either retrained or replaced. Which leads to the obvious question: How can you tell whether or not you've got—or, if you're the current leader yourself reading this, you *are*—the right person for the task? Here are some questions to ask that may be helpful.

*Is the current leader a genuinely spiritual person?* Do they genuinely walk with Jesus and desire others—most notably students—to do the same? Are they notably filled with the Spirit of God? Remember, the transformation that God desires for our schools is first and foremost a spiritual one. Without a genuine relationship with Christ, the most gifted leader on the planet will fail at guiding one of our schools back into true health—period.

*Is the current leader passionate about Adventism?* Do I really need to explain this one?

*Is the current leader a visionary leader?* That is, can he or she picture what that bright, healthy future for your school looks like and convey it to others in a coherent, compelling way?

*Is the current leader someone who highly values both personal and corporate accountability?* Being willing to be held answerable to the school board, conference, etc., and, in turn, being willing to hold whatever staff members are at the school responsible for making needed changes, is indispensable to transforming a school that's fallen on hard times. (In fact, a distinct lack of accountability is often key to a school's demise in the first place.)

*Is the current leader trusted by an appropriate range of his or her constituents?* Trust is a leader's stock-in-trade. If a he or she doesn't have it, that leader's ability to affect change will be minimal at best.

*Is the current leader one who has already been pushing aggressively for reform?* Ah, fundamental question here! Good leaders of transformation generally don't wait for better opportunities before they start casting a vision for a brighter tomorrow. They may be limited in their success by uncooperative school boards or parents, but they will already be agitating for reform whether they receive support in that quest or not.

The truth is that if a leader of a declining school is not actively and aggressively campaigning for appropriate changes already, that individual is probably part of the problem rather than its solution. Which leads to a difficult decision: Should a school retrain or replace such a leader?

Obviously it is not a question that can be answered in a book. Use God's guidance, your own wisdom, and local context to make that call. However, note that visionary, transformational leadership is very difficult to teach to someone who lacks it—and that problem only increases when a school's situation has reached crisis mode. If retraining is your only option, then set up clear lines of communication, clearly defined goals, clear lines of accountability, and go for it. On the other hand, if retraining seems ill advised or if the leader is unwilling, replacement may indeed be the better option.

## The Role of Upper-Level Administration in Leadership Development

Here we encounter an interesting fork in the road. We've been talking about how to deal with renewal on the local level. But for just a moment we need to jump to the conference and union (or higher?). Here's why: My guess is that experienced educators/administrators/board members reading the thoughts on leadership in this book may have already shaken their heads and said, "Well, of *course* we need the right leaders at our schools. But do you have any idea how hard it is to *find* them today? If I could just snap my fingers and get great leaders in response, all this wouldn't be an issue, now, would it?"

Point well taken. Finding quality leaders for Adventist schools is a huge problem in the NAD. For instance, recently the principal's position at one of our prominent academies came open. The search committee asked many competent leaders to consider the job—not to take the job, mind you, just to consider it. *More than 20 of them said no*, and at last check, the school had given up looking outside for leadership and had instead sought to fill the post from within. *More than 20 administrators, specifically contacted about a post at a school that has a solid reputation, would not even consider the job!*

And thus we meet head-on one of the biggest obstacles to turning the tide in Adventist education: Few people want to be a principal anymore, much less a transformational one. The pay is too low, the stress is too high, and the decisions to be made to have a healthy school are politically and personally often costly ones. It's a very difficult task to do, and few indeed are those volunteering for the job.

But that fact doesn't alter our need for great principals or other school leaders. So what to do? At the local level, we can retrain current leaders (if possible) or recruit quality local leadership (if available). But to really address the leadership vacuum at the local level, upper church administration will have to become involved, something I'll address at length in chapter 19.

## A Final Leadership Question

Finally, a most basic question that we must ask of the current school head:

*Is the current administrator a skilled leader?* As most of us know, a title doth not a leader make. Leadership is certainly part art, but it also includes a basic skill set. Such leaders need to be able to run effective meetings, establish appropriate priorities and address them in that order, set a reasonable pace in the life of the school, interact with students and constituents well, return phone calls in a timely fashion, communicate effectively concerning the core competencies of the school, hold students and staff appropriately account-able, and so forth. Without such skills even visionary leadership will falter. But with them vision can become reality.

A final note for those of you new to the search for school leaders. If you are in the market for one, how do you find the right individual for your school? Well, as mentioned above, we need a systemic fix at the upper levels of church administration before obtaining such people will become any-thing approaching easy (again, more on this in chapter 19). But until then, getting the person you need for your school may come down to two things: listening to the Spirit's guiding, and sheer determination. In other words, *pray fervently for the right person*, and then *ask everyone you can think of for sug-gestions*. Use the ACG (that's "Adventist communication grapevine," of course) to your advantage and make phone calls far and wide. Start with principals you know of who've led their schools through transformation successfully—they often can suggest other like-minded individuals who may be able to come to your school. Call old friends from college to see whom they know of that fits your school's situation; e-mail all your relatives; men-tion your needs to anyone who will listen (and even to some who won't!). God has someone out there for your school, but you may have to dig for them. Don't give up till you've found the right one.

# CHAPTER 13

# Step 4:
# Discover the
# True State of Your School

B ut I already know the condition of my school!" you might be saying.
"We're dying—what more do I need to know than that?" Potentially, a
great deal.

Recognizing that your school is in trouble and realizing *why* it is can be
two very distinct things. I illustrated this earlier with the issue of tuition
being "too expensive": the reality is that it may be—or it may not be. Here's
where specific, measurable research will tell you for sure one way or the
other, with the same being true for most other causative factors in Adventist educational decline.

So what to do? Again, it's simple: Audit your school, and in as many
ways as appropriate.

One way to do this is to have an outside team of skilled educators and
administrators inspect your school's program from top to bottom. Ask them
to come for several days, giving them complete access to everything you do,
from curriculum, to finances, to student life, to scheduling—whatever. Request them to interview students, their parents, and staff, inviting their opinions about the school, what ails it, and how to fix it. Also, if your school is
attached to a constituent church or churches, have your audit team meet
with their boards (or at least a sampling of them) to get their input.

The audit team may include your local conference superintendent of
education and his or her assistants, and you will probably also want to include
several people who have no current interaction with your school or possibly even your conference. The latter group, while they may miss some of the
finer points of your program because of their newness, will undoubtedly for
that same reason spot flaws that locals might miss.

After the audit team has studied your school for the appropriate time (larger primary and secondary schools may require four or five days, colleges and universities more), meet with them to hear their conclusions. Consider them seriously, and take appropriate action based on those findings.

SVA commissioned an outside auditing team to examine the school during the winter of the 2007-2008 school year—less than six months after the dramatic drop of 70 students in enrollment. The team consisted of experienced educators and administrators, some currently working at successful Adventist academies. As prescribed above, the auditors received complete access to all facets of the school. Their findings were helpful in both revealing new weaknesses and confirming ones suspected previously.

A brief aside on the notion of accreditation may be helpful here. All Adventist schools must be accredited on a regular basis by the appropriate accrediting body. Such accreditations require some sort of self-study, as well as the visit of an accreditation team. Like the auditing team described above, they also look for strengths and weaknesses in a given school in a quest to help it improve. The similarities in function may lead some to conclude, "Well, we were audited by the accreditation team and received our accreditation, so the true state of our school must be one of health—even though our enrollment is terrible."

Ironically, most of the schools that have closed over the past 20 years were fully accredited when they shut down.

Could it be that we need to improve our accreditation practices so that our schools can better know their true condition and make appropriate adjustments before it's too late? Having been personally involved in the accreditation self-study process at the primary, secondary, and postgraduate levels, I believe the answer is solidly yes. While the current system does an excellent job at assessing *what* a school is doing (teaching this part of Bible, this part of science, this part of English, etc.), it does not have a sufficient metric for determining whether or not a school is an *excellent* school. But this is crucial! We live in a world in which God, Ellen White, and yes, current culture all call for the absolute best for our children. Sloppiness may be OK for farm animals, but when it comes to our kids, every parent wants the most excellent education available. It is thus not enough that a school teaches the appropriate sections of Bible—it must do so with excellence, with a striving to conduct discipleship of students in the most effective and engaging way possible. It's not enough just to offer a full science program. We must present that complete course with the best methods available and with an eye toward giving students an absolute relish for the sciences and the God who established them. Excellence will define a truly Adventist school, and it's time that our accreditation process supports that fact.

Though inferior to the outside auditing team method, another way to gain a more accurate picture of your school is simply to take a mass survey. True, this idea will work better in some schools than in others, so use your judgment. But if it does seem advisable, then poll all available involved people about what's right and wrong with the institution and how they would suggest fixing the problems. It means asking staff, faculty, students, parents, board members, and other constituents for their honest input. Be prepared for some answers that are shortsighted and inaccurate (the education of children can often evoke strong emotions that may cloud otherwise sound judgment and thus affect the quality of some answers). However, some gems will rise to the surface, and those are the answers you're looking for. Grab them and use them appropriately.

The thought of taking an open-questioned survey about your school's health may seem scary to some and unnecessary to others. Those who are frightened may believe that people will use it as a weapon, unleashing, for instance, their pent-up frustrations on the already-suffering school-teachers. That is entirely possible. But you can minimize the danger by stating clearly at the beginning of the survey what its intent is—to find viable solutions, not to tear down faculty or staff. Those who see such survey work as unnecessary may believe that they already know what's wrong with their school and that conducting one would just be an unnecessary delay in the reform process—and they may be correct! But before dismissing completely the survey idea, consider two things. First, the principal or school board or parent who has the *entire* picture of their school's needs already in their head is a rare bird indeed. Not often does any one person get all the pieces of the puzzle in their box—thus, there is usually wisdom in a multitude of counselors. Second, when you ask for other people's input into turning your school around via a survey, you also give them an opportunity to buy in personally to the process—and that can prove to be very valuable indeed.

## A Word on the Power of Myth

I cannot end discussion on step 4 in the change process without driving home the "power of myth"—that is, the ability of otherwise good people to persist in thinking that "our school is OK" even with clear evidence to the contrary. When you're trying to discover the true state of your school, mythology is a deadly trap that will immediately and continually stifle your efforts to change.

So how can you avoid buying into mythology? One of the best ways is to expose yourself (and as many staff, administrators, etc., as possible) to the best: the best schools, the best administrators, the best leaders. For instance, if you're not sure about the extent of the decline at your school or exactly what's wrong with it, find the best example of your type (elementary, secondary, etc.) and visit it (and no, it needn't necessarily be Adventist—while keeping our Adventist core, we can learn a lot from others who come at education with a different bent). Spend several days at that school or schools. Conduct interviews (with permission, of course) with its students, parents, teachers, and administrators. Ask lots of questions about how they do things, why, what mistakes they've made, what are their successes, and so forth. Learn from them all that you can. You see, too often, unless we "get out of Mayberry" every now and then, we begin to think that our corner of the world is actually the world. Exposure to world-class education can change all that for the better, and it will help you *really* to learn the actual condition of your school.

In whatever way you go about it, determining the true state of your school is absolutely crucial to fixing what ails it. Remember, Jesus' statement that "you shall know the truth, and the truth shall set you free" (see John 8:32) applies to more than personal salvation—it includes our schools, too. Discover the truth about your school, and you'll be that much closer to turning it back to the "freedom" that only health and vibrancy can bring.

# CHAPTER 14

# Step 5:
# Master the Fundamentals
# of Adventist Education

There are other good books on this topic,[1] and I'm not going to try to reproduce them here. So before I give a brief listing of Adventist educational fundamentals and their descriptions, we need to consider a specific point.

When it comes to the local school's role in their own decline, my experience is that most of our schools that are in bad shape too often have slipped into that condition because of a poor grasp of what they should be. In other words, the school that has declined because of a freak accident (town industry closing down and population subsequently vanishing overnight, a fire or flood wiping out their buildings, a meteor striking the ad building, etc.) is rare indeed. Far more prevalent are those that have simply let themselves go in regard to the fundamentals.

If you'll allow me another sports analogy, the star players in the National Basketball Association make a lot of headlines in the news and generate more than their fair share of ticket sales. However, when the whistle blows and the actual game begins, the team who has mastered the principles of the sport—whether they have a star player on their side or not—will nearly always prevail. NBA promoters are loath to talk about this fact, probably because it's not a very flashy reality ("Dribble and pass the ball well and you'll win a title" seems to lack a certain panache). But it has been shown to be the case again and again.

The same is true for our schools, only more so. If our schools can master the following list of Adventist education fundamentals—that is, do them with excellence—we too will "win the championship," and the population of our schools will come to reflect that fact. A quality product will draw in Adventist (and occasionally other) parents, and a quality product requires mastering the basics.

Here's a partial listing of those fundamentals:

1. *Student salvation.* As described previously, the primary goal of an Adventist school is for each of its students to develop a saving relationship with Jesus. All that an educational institution does needs to contribute somehow to this primary goal. Any program or activity that detracts from that purpose must be corrected or else eliminated as soon as possible.

2. *Safety.* We live in a world different from the one we did 10 years ago. The events of September 11, Columbine, and other tragedies have pressed the "bubble generation" of parents to protect their kids from all manner of actual or potential threats. Your school must reflect that reality. The grounds must be safe from unwanted outside entry. The administration should have zero tolerance toward deadly weapons, drug use, fighting, bullying, and sexual activity. In the classroom teachers must make clear what they expect of students and be consistent in their enforcement of those requirements. Rules should be as few as possible (not necessarily few, just as few as possible) and consistently applied. Schools that master this fundamental are grace-oriented, yet are not afraid to expel students who violate known zero-tolerance standards. (Too often in the past we have confused student enrollment with student salvation. Kicking misbehaving young people out of school after they have violated clearly stated zero-tolerance rules is not the same as throwing them out of the kingdom of God. Those students can and do still enter the kingdom of heaven, while at the same time their absence from campus frees other students from a potentially damaging influence.)

3. *High-quality academics.* We have already spent some time on this back in chapter 7. Building on the concerns addressed there, every school needs to ask itself at least the following questions:

Do we have empirical proof that our academic study program is of high quality?

Are our students being more than adequately prepared for the next step in their academic journey (an academy, enrollment in college or in a university)?

Do our students enjoy learning? How do we know that?

Are parents so impressed with our academic program that they willingly tell others about its quality?

Do we have regular methods of evaluating and improving our academic program?

As I mentioned in chapter 7, I believe that many parents are no longer interested in their kids' merely equaling or mildly exceeding public school students academically. They instead want to surpass them by a sizable margin. But whatever the desires of various parents may be, academic excellence is an important fundamental to master in your school.

*4. High-quality teachers and staff.* Consider this statement: "Teachers and staff are key links between God and students." Is it true? I believe so, particularly in primary and secondary level settings. How about this one: "Teachers and staff are the key links between students and academic excellence." Again, I think it is clearly the case. Low-quality teachers and staff can lead to academic—and most ominously, salvific—failure. *A school will rise no higher than the quality of its teachers and staff.*

So if your school is currently employing great teachers and staff, praise the Lord! Do everything you can to retain them. Reward them, both publicly and privately. Let them know you consider it an honor to work with them. Give them gifts that let them know you appreciate them (and no, it doesn't always have to be high dollar to be high impact—just something to express your appreciation). Find ways to pay for them to take advantage of high-quality continuing education opportunities. Motivate them to continue to grow (great staff and teachers will respond to positive challenges, not cower from them). Back them up when they come under pressure from others. In other words, treat high-quality staff and teachers like what they are, and they will continue to be high-quality staff and teachers.

On the other hand, our schools also have some not-so-high quality staff and teachers. Where appropriate, some can be retrained and can contribute to the school's program. Most administrators will know the various ways to do this, but I'll mention them here for the sake of those who may not be familiar with them, using the retraining of a poorly performing teacher as the example.

Retraining teachers revolves around one word: accountability. All teachers serve in the Adventist system because, at the very least, they have agreed to uphold certain standards and adhere to a particular mission (or at least, it *ought* to be the case). We must clearly articulate such standards and mission in a face-to-face meeting between teachers and administrator/school leader(s). Poorly performing teachers need to be told clearly that their performance is unacceptable and (if called for) that their employment is potentially at stake because of it. To continue in their teaching role they must improve in specific, measurable ways. But to establish what they are, administration must outline clear performance criteria and set time lines for when those various standards should be met and mastered. The school must establish paths of communication between the teachers and their supervisors (phone, e-mail, face-to-face), as well as how those paths will function in the retraining process. At the agreed-upon deadlines the school will again review the teacher's performance, documenting any advances made or still needed. If the teacher improves, praise the Lord! The teacher—and your school—will advance commensurately. However, if after (a) the teacher fails to adhere to the new expectations after receiving an appropriate amount of time and if after (b) the administrator has made the appropriate documentation of that lack of progress (check your local union education code for specifics on this time period and documentation required), then the school need not renew that teacher's contract for the following school year.

This may seem like Administration 101 to many of you, but if it is, Administration 101 too often gets ignored. The general rule in my experience is that shoddy instruction is not only tolerated but actually reinforced through continually renewing the contracts of subpar teachers. "But accountability and retraining take time!" we complain. Yes, that's true. It's also true that terminating a teacher is *never* enjoyable and often exceedingly painful. But that doesn't change the fact that even greater pain results when we repeatedly inflict poor teachers on our kids whose future life success—and possibly salvation—hangs in the balance.

A few final points on maintaining or developing high-quality staff:

First, all teaching staff—whether they're good, bad, or indifferent—require regular evaluations. The good teachers welcome it, the bad ones put on their best face, and the indifferent ones are, well, indifferent to the evaluation process. But they *all* need it, and that's why union education codes demand it. Periodic evaluations are the only way to establish accountability for high standards in our schools (perhaps that's why the education code stipulates them?). Don't skip regular evaluations of your staff!

Second, as you're able to, offer regular access to quality continuing education opportunities. Everyone gets in a rut sometimes. Be responsible for pulling your teachers and staff out of such traps, reinvigorating them with fresh ideas, and helping them regain high quality performance.

Last, when it comes to mastering the fundamental of having high-quality teachers and staff, note the following maxim: *This fundamental can't be faked.* Your teachers and staff may be able to pretend for a short while that they're the real deal. But if you've got poor-quality people in your school, it will show sooner or later—guaranteed, with no exceptions. Woe to the principal or school board who thinks a repeatedly recalcitrant employee should stay regardless of poor performance! And great joy to the principal or school board who regularly expect, plan for, and foster high-quality performance from teachers and staff, for their schools will have the best chance of beating the odds and moving into health.

5. *Strong work ethic.* With the challenges of childhood obesity and sedentary lifestyles, the need for teaching children the fundamental skill of hard work may be one of the greatest that students have. Regardless of the grade levels your school instructs, all students should learn the value of hard work in profitable (morally and/or financially) pursuits. And, in my opinion, such work opportunities ought to be mandatory, not elective—that is, *every student in every Adventist school—even at the college level—ought to have some form of compulsory labor in addition to their academic studies that helps to instill in them a strong work ethic.*

Again, this is not rocket science. In fact, most elementary school teachers already do this, assigning daily and weekly chores to their students, tasks that range from taking out the trash to cleaning off desktops to pulling weeds in the front flowerbeds. However, when high school rolls around, many schools lay off the required student labor. Yet the work possibilities for that age group are more varied and certainly no less needed than for their elementary student counterparts. High school students can (and should) be assigned to and trained in more skill-intensive areas of work, such as physical plant maintenance; farming (if the resources are available) or other forms of husbandry; being a reader (grader), a spiritual and social mentor to younger kids, or a student senator; or working in partnership with local businesses that employ them at their site (health care facilities, restaurants, etc.). Last but not least, college students obviously have the greatest potential for engaging in meaningful work, particularly as they gear up for their future careers.

Students must learn more than just facts. They also must experience *fervor* and *perseverance*—dedication to a worthwhile task *until it is done*. This will serve them well in the job market and in the service of the Lord, and thus is another fundamental that we must master if our schools are to thrive.

6. *Instilling passion for the unique mission of the Adventist Church.* I've dedicated quite a bit of ink to the importance of this fundamental already, and with good reason. If you don't master it, you can have all the "success" in the world and still be unfaithful to the calling that God has given the *Adventist* Church. Adventist education ought regularly to instill great passion for the Advent movement and its mission, which can be done in at least the following ways:

a. *Get the first fundamental—a relationship with Jesus—done right at the very beginning.*

b. *Make sure that your curriculum holds up the Bible as the ultimate guide for life and service.* Every academic discipline ought to be able to do this. Whether they teach Bible, auto mechanics, physics, or whatever, every teacher ought to be able to incorporate the Bible into their classroom instruction.[2] It may be as simple as reading a text or two followed by a brief personal thought at the beginning of each class, or (better yet) including during classroom discussion Bible references that tie in to the topic being presented. However it's done, students should be able to assume that their teachers hold the Bible in high esteem, and that personally and professionally it is their guide for faith and practice.

c. *Teach students about the unique mission of the Adventist Church, including its specific doctrines.* This might seem like a no-brainer, but it most certainly is not. For instance, while division-wide standards govern the Bible curriculum for primary and secondary Adventist schools, I have yet to have contact with one that wasn't deviating in some significant ways from that curriculum. I've been at K–8 schools in which the principals pointed out that at no time in those nine grades did students receive any specific instruction about the Sabbath. I've visited academies where students received some instruction (much of it well done) on key Adventist doctrines, but had virtually no grasp of Adventism's unique mission in the world or how to carry it out. And beyond our primary and secondary schools, I've visited colleges in which, as I mentioned previously, any unique facets of Adventism were so muted as to be essentially invisible and uninspiring.

If your school is in decline and you want it to thrive again, you must overcome such oversights. Do not be shy about your church in your class-rooms. It's an honor to be called by God to be an Adventist, and your cur-riculum must tangibly show that. Which brings us to another key need.

d. *Hire staff that are passionate Adventists.* The old saying is true: Passion is more caught than taught. It's nearly impossible for teachers bored or even antagonistic toward Adventism to produce graduates who are any-thing but bored or antagonistic toward Adventism. But hire passionate Ad-ventists, and passionate Adventist grads are much more likely to come from your school.

e. *Whenever possible, have students bring the unique Adventist message and mission into contact with real life.* Have them go on short-term mission trips, either around the block or around the world somewhere. Enable them to teach others personally about Jesus' soon return—and then actually create sit-uations in which they can do just that: branch Sabbath schools, after-school programs, student-run Revelation seminars or other evangelistic series, per-sonal Bible studies in the community, etc. Give students opportunities to share their uniquely Adventist faith with others, and in so doing, not only will the kingdom of God grow but even more your students. *But you've got to make it real, hands-on,* not just theory taught in the classroom.

f. *Appropriately integrate the writings of Adventist history and Ellen White into the lives of your students.* During the first 12 years of my exclusively Adventist education my teachers never assigned me a single book by Ellen White. True, they encouraged me to read a couple excerpts from *The Desire of Ages* and *Steps to Christ,* but that was it. And as far as being taught about Adventist his-tory, I picked up a few facts here and there, but never had anything even re-motely comprehensive until college—and then it required only a single class (appropriately titled "History of Adventism" and wonderfully taught by one of my favorite professors, Alden Thompson). One class, and that was only because I was a theology major!

Now, granted, that was back in the early 1990s. But in my experience, too often the same attitude stubbornly persists today that says "Adventist his-tory is passé and boring, and we cannot afford to sedate our students with such antiquated material."

Passé? Boring? Only those who know very little about Adventist history could ever arrive at such a conclusion. The development of God's last-day movement on earth, designed to help usher in the very end of human history, is one of the most riveting stories in recent history. The sacrifice of our pioneers,[3] the miracles that God performed to advance the church along, its incredible global growth—all of this and more make the account of the Adventist Church one that is truly gripping.

And by the way, there's also this woman named Ellen White, who just happened to be a prophet of God and lived within the past 100 years. She; her husband, James; and an old sea captain named Joseph Bates started the Adventist Church. Jesus spoke with Ellen, and she spoke with Jesus face to face—and last I checked, that doesn't happen to many people, not only in the past 100 years, but in the past 1,000! Think carefully: Whom do you know that has had 2,000 credible visions from the Almighty? Short list, isn't it? The point, then, should be clear: *Ellen White's writings are a treasure trove awaiting rediscovery by the Adventist Church, the very group that she helped found.* The inspired counsel her books contain represent a profound escalation of God's activity on earth in preparation for the second coming of Jesus Christ, and here we sit, too often making excuses for her writings when actually we should be reading them, studying them, and seeking how best to apply them in our and our students' lives.

Let me make one final point in deference to those who do not find the writings of Ellen White as much boring or passé as they do inflammatory and dangerous—and yes, legalistic. Many thoughtful authors have written over the years on this very topic, and I'll not try to repeat their arguments here. I would simply say that it seems reasonable that after 160 years of experience with the prophetic gift of Ellen White, we ought to be able to present her writings both passionately *and* in a balanced fashion. Will some teachers and schools make mistakes and miss that balance—one direction or the other? Count on it. But I would rather see our schools take that risk and attempt to deal honestly with Ellen White's writings than I would have them hide her books under lock and key, muting God's witness to our church through her gift. Our schools need to teach our students the story of Adventist history and expose them to the prophetic corpus of writings. Such things are indispensable to instilling passion for the unique Adventist mission in your students.

g. *Live out the apocalyptic mind-set of genuine Adventism in front of students.*

This recommendation is at the core of what is required to instill passion for the unique mission of the Adventist Church. It is also one of the things that I believe our church at large is in danger of losing.

A little background may be helpful here. Since our beginnings in the mid-1800s, we Adventists have had to deal with the tension of the "now" and the "not yet" facets of Christ's second coming. On the one hand, Bible prophecy, the writings of Ellen White, and world events of the past 160-plus years have regularly lent themselves to the conclusion that Jesus' "return is just around the corner"—almost now! On the other hand, Jesus' return has been "just around the corner" for, well, more than 160 years! But it has not yet occurred.

The tension is obvious. What's a thinking Adventist—or more to the point, the thinking Adventist school—to do?

The following points are ones that I've found personally compelling in regard to the "now" and the "not yet" and how that plays out in resolving the tension surrounding Christ's return.

1. The expectation of Christ's return—the longing to see our Savior as soon as possible—is indispensable to being a Seventh-day Adventist. You cannot be a healthy Seventh-day Adventist (nor, some would argue, any other brand of Christian) and *not* have this desire!

2. Yet we are not to live on "time excitement." In other words, one reason that we're Adventists should be that we want Jesus to come soon—but not that we insist He arrive on, say, June 10 of next year. No matter how compelling current events may get, date setting—even date setting of a general nature ("within the next six months!" for instance) is unbiblical and counterproductive.

3. However, simply because "no man knows the day nor the hour" (see Matt. 24:36) does not mean that we are clueless as to the signs occurring all around us that indicate that Christ's return is indeed sooner rather than later. We thus find ourselves called neither to fanatical date setting nor to complacent dismissiveness, but rather to steady, passionate watching and working for the soon return of Christ—regardless of how Jesus chooses to define "soon." "Watch, therefore, lest the Son of Man come at an hour that you do not expect him," Jesus said (see verse 44).

And what does this mean for a school that wants to instill passion for the unique mission of the Adventist Church? It requires at the very least that we ask some key questions and answer them appropriately:

Do our students understand the potential nearness of the coming of Christ? If not, how will we educate them to grasp this?

Do our students conduct themselves, make decisions for the future, etc., in light of the fact that Jesus may return in their lifetime? If not, how can we help them to think in this way?

Do our students graduate with a passion to see Jesus come in their lifetime, as well as a drive to enable others to be ready for that great event? If not, how will we instill in them such concern?

Do our school board and staff members live with a joyful sense of the nearness of Christ's coming? Are the decisions they make done in light of that awareness? Do they approach the future with any serious regard for the thought that says "We will do thus and so . . . if time shall last that long"? If not, what changes do we need to see that spirit revived in our school?

For the schools that have the courage to ask and answer these questions honestly—and to follow through with the necessary changes in their educational program the answers call for—their chances for being a vibrant Adventist institutions for Christ are commensurately greater.

7. *Parent user-friendliness.* Don't let the placement of this fundamental last on the list fool you. Every quality Adventist school must have clearly defined channels of communication between school faculty (teachers, principal, staff) and parents. To be blunt, *this is huge.* If a parent calls the school, for instance, someone—as in, an actual person—should ideally pick up the phone first or (if you have an automated directory) within a very short time of the call being placed. Parents who have questions or requests about grades, transcripts, tuition bills, policies, or anything else need to have clear paths delineated for them by school administration through which they can have their concerns addressed. Teachers must be reasonably accessible for parents to talk to. In this day and age when communication methods are advanced but school employee's calendars are often overly full, our educational institutions that want to succeed must nonetheless make parents a top priority. If you don't make your school user-friendly for your parents, they—and their students—will go elsewhere, period. Vibrant or wanting-to-be-vibrant schools accept this and employ whatever steps necessary to accomplish it.

A final thought on user-friendliness: This fundamental is unique in that, if a school really starts to hit the skids, open communication with parents is often one of the first things to go. The institution goes into fortress mode and carefully regulates information—particularly bad news. Parents who begin to get suspicious start phoning, but those calls sometimes do not get returned in a timely fashion, or even at all. Communication grinds to a standstill. And what's ironic is that *such restrictions often result from the assumption that less communication with parents will actually help the school get better.*

Of course, in reality the opposite is true. Though there may be the rare exception, most parents don't want to see the school their child attends tank either. And many times they have good suggestions to share with teachers and administration that will help solve some of the school's problems . . . but only if they have the ability to present those suggestions successfully!

Make your school user-friendly to the parents. They—and your enrollment office—will thank you.

## Hey, What About MVA and SVA?

It's been a few pages since we left our two school examples. Both institutions and their rejuvenation process could speak volumes when it comes to mastering the fundamentals of Adventist education. But in the interest of brevity, I'll make just two observations.

First, both academies have had to make huge strides in the area of the fundamentals. Every fundamental area listed above has required extensive work to raise performance to appropriate standards. When you're turning around a school for the glory of God, expect to do a lot of work in the basics!

Second, while great progress has been made, neither MVA nor SVA has arrived when it comes to mastering educational fundamentals. Excellence is a journey, not a destination, and I can guarantee you that both principals currently present at either school could give you a quick listing of where they're pushing mightily to improve. Consequently, the key for them—and possible for you, too—is to reach a solid level of proficiency with each fundamental, and then relentlessly improve upon them. That's what an excellent Adventist school thrives on—mastered fundamentals, consistently improved upon through time.

[1] Again, Ellen White's book *Education* is a great place to start.

[2] This is not a call to repeat the mistake of Battle Creek College more than a century ago in which some faculty pushed for the Bible to be the textbook in every class—including the sciences and even accounting! Instead, it is a recognition that the Bible is foundational and normative for all Christians, regardless of their future or current vocations or avocations.

[3] See Jim Nix, ed., *The Spirit of Sacrifice and Commitment,* for some fantastic stories of the early Adventist pioneers.

# CHAPTER 15

# Step 6:
# Relentlessly Eliminate
# Weaknesses or Make Them Irrelevant

The pursuit of the mastery of the fundamentals of Adventist education will have a number of positive results. But one of the most important is the revealing of weaknesses.

For instance, if your academic program has been subpar and you then begin to try to raise the bar to where it needs to be, you will quickly discover exactly what your program is lacking. For example, teachers may not have the certification required to teach at the level of excellence you require. Or your physical plant may be in such poor repair that it defies your efforts to have a safe learning environment. Whatever the case, finding weaknesses is—uncomfortable though it may be—one of the most valuable journeys you can take when seeking to right your school.

Unfortunately, most people avoid bad news if at all possible. And as for actually seeking out problems—"bad news"—and listing them and dissecting them? That can seem like odd (and potentially most unwelcome) behavior indeed.

But if you're going to return your school to the vibrancy that God intends for it, you must relentlessly seek out its weaknesses and then deal with them. You need to tell the truth about your school. Or call in others to explain it. Do whatever it takes by whatever means are ethical and appropriate to find out the true state of your school and what its weaknesses are.

And what do you do with them when you find them? You have really only three options:

1. Change nothing. Many schools have chosen this option, and some of them are closed or in the process of shutting down as a result (see chapter 8 for more details on the success of this plan).

2. Eliminate the weakness, or, if that is not feasible:

3. Make the weakness irrelevant.

Let's assume that you wisely avoid option 1 and want to choose from the remaining two. How do you know whether to eliminate a weakness or simply make it irrelevant? And if you do decide to make it irrelevant, how do you do that?

First of all, let's state the obvious: As much as possible, *always eliminate your weaknesses in the fundamentals*. If you have a poor academic program, for instance, fix it. Don't try to mildly modify it or shore up other portions of your program to cover for this major flaw. Fix the weakness in any fundamental. Tell staff members, board members, constituents, and everyone else that it is a nonnegotiable, that this weakness must be eliminated because *it is a fundamental and cannot be made irrelevant*. It is often better to shut down an Adventist school that perpetually cannot fix its weaknesses in the fundamentals than it is to carry on, pretending to offer a quality Adventist education when actually it most certainly does not. Solve those fundamental problems at all costs! (And by the way—perhaps in no other single area is the rightness or wrongness of your school leader illustrated more graphically than in his or her ability to identify basic problems and fix them. If the person consistently cannot do this, you have the wrong leader in your school. They need either retraining or replacement as soon as possible.)

One of the fundamental weaknesses that both MVA and SVA had when Twomley became principal was in the area of academics. For a variety of reasons (attributable to no single source), this area needed help. So both schools quickly implemented dual credit programs. They allowed qualified students to take college-credit classes while fulfilling the graduation requirements for high school. The results have been very satisfying, and some MVA grads have even had enough credits to start college as a sophomore rather than a freshman. Not only does it give mom and dad a break at the bank (having one less year of college to pay for)—it also sends a strong message to constituents of both schools: We are eliminating a key weakness by being dedicated to academic excellence.

But what about weaknesses in nonfundamental areas? For instance, some physical plant issues may not qualify as a fundamental concern (unless things are so bad that it involves a student safety question, of course). Issues such as food service quality, certain student behavioral policies, bill collection pro-cedures, registration practices, and so forth may also not fall under the ban-ner of "fundamental," even though the areas involved may indicate genuine weaknesses. What to do with these types of issues?

Again, if you have the option, fix them. Prioritize the weaknesses as which to address first, assess what you need to do to take care of it, and do it.

But let's say that you don't have the resources necessary to deal with the weakness right away. If that's the case, choose option 3 and do your best to make the weakness irrelevant to the success of your school. There are at least two ways to accomplish that: (1) through *mitigation* and (2) through *truth-telling*. As we'll see, neither of them is complicated. But for those unfamiliar with such practices, let's briefly go through them.

Making a weakness irrelevant through mitigation is always the better option if you have a choice. Your goal here is not to eliminate the weakness completely (since, if you're taking this step, I'm assuming that's not possible), but at least to remove it *partially*, to make changes that will reduce its impact on the overall program of your school.

For instance, at SVA one of their great strengths is also a weakness: They're located in New Market, Virginia, a little town of 1,700 residents far from any large metro area. But those large metro areas are the very ones that the majority of SVA's conference constituents live in. So while it's a great lo-cation for being away from city life, parents who live in, say, the Washington, D.C., area who are considering enrolling their freshmen or sophomore chil-dren may consider it *too far* away. For those parents, the thought of having their youngsters living in a new and distant school away from home for weeks at a time can overwhelm them.

Clearly, it is not a weakness that can be easily eliminated. So instead, SVA has mitigated it. It has instituted a partial boarding program in which every weekend (except for closed weekends), transportation is available for freshmen and sophomore dorm students to go home. Thus, while SVA is still out in the boonies, parents are now able to make the transition to their kids being so far away more gently and over time. The weakness of distance remains, but it is now increasingly irrelevant.

Other schools have created similar solutions. For instance, at Newbury Park Academy in southern California, longtime administrator Harold Crook reinstituted a campus living arrangement after their dorms had remained closed for many years. Most people would consider this a step backwards and a reviving of some old perceived weaknesses—namely, that boarding students are (1) removed from their parents for weeks on end and (2) run wild during that time because of minimal supervision. But Mr. Crook succeeded in making those old weaknesses irrelevant and even strengths through using on-campus homes with on-campus parents living in them. This allowed students to live at their "home" on campus—with adequate supervision—during the school week and then drive to their real homes on the weekends, minimizing the time of separation from parents. The results speak for themselves. Prior to instituting the on-campus home program Newbury was a day school with about 120 students. As I write this, they have approximately 200. The school made its particular weakness insignificant.

A second way to make a weakness irrelevant is through truth-telling. No, this does not assume that you've been lying about your school thus far! Rather, truth-telling entails *being honest about your weaknesses and trumpeting your strengths*. And coupled with appropriate mitigation efforts, truth-telling can have very beneficial results.

Constituents have a right to know the workings of your school, including its problems. But they also need to the know the truth, which might go something like this: "In spite of our school's weaknesses in _____ and _____, the overall program is still strong/becoming stronger, and here's the evidence to prove it."

Obviously, you could not honestly make such a statement if your school has just begun its change process (this again is why the elimination of weaknesses in the fundamentals should precede efforts to make weaknesses irrelevant). But in most sincere and informed change efforts, at least *some* good things begin to happen in the school fairly quickly. Trumpet them. Let the Lord use them as seeds in constituents' minds from which He can grow increasing enthusiasm for supporting your school (more on this in chapter 16). Continue to be honest about your weaknesses, while also being up-front about your successes.

This brings up a key leadership principle often overlooked by schools seeking to return to vibrancy: Be honest about negative things. Too many times, struggling institutions have a nearly insurmountable urge to "put a happy face" on things, to talk brightly about the school's future, trying to be optimistic, even though in actuality the school is teetering on the edge of closing. Such optimism might be laudable under other circumstances, but here it is a potentially catastrophic liability. *When your school is doing poorly and others can readily see it and you nonetheless persist in seeing things through rose-colored glasses, you cannot help appearing deeply incompetent.*

But the converse is also true, at least a great deal of the time.* While it may not always make them happy, people generally admire a leader who can correctly identify the true condition of their kids' school. The facts are that parents generally prefer knowing about the weaknesses of your institution. Furthermore, they prefer the information about them to come from the school (preferably the principal, school president, or lead teacher), as opposed to from the gossip circuit or even from their own child. If you're actively working to revive your school—and if you've made the change effort public enough that parents can see it—such truth-telling on your part usually makes your stock go up, not down! Tell the truth about your weaknesses while working hard to trumpet the truth about your strengths. Done correctly, this can have a positive and snowball effect on the revitalization program at your school, which we'll talk more about in the next chapter.

---

*True, some school administrators have been fired for telling the truth about their schools. The board/constituents/conference/whoever did not appreciate the message, so they shot the messenger. This is a difficult reality. But at the very least—and I do not say this flippantly—those that have been fired for truth-telling can sleep better at night, knowing that they did what they could to save the school from tanking. They also have the assurance that God will take care of them, as He needs truth-tellers in many places.

# CHAPTER 16

# Step 7:
# Get the Good Word Out/
# Enlist Widespread Support

This chapter builds on the truth-telling efforts of a school attempting to deal effectively with its weaknesses. Specifically, it seeks to answer the question, How can a school that's pulling out of decline build widespread momentum among its constituency that will assist in making the change effort successful?

As with other steps in the transformation process, this one is not complicated. But it is time-consuming and requires—depending on the size of a school and its constituency—significant outlays of time and energy.

Before I touch on what you should spend that time and energy on, I should note that this seventh step in the school revitalization process is very tempting to skip, precisely because it demands so much time and energy. Usually, change efforts are difficult enough to accomplish on a purely intraschool level without having also to engage the wider constituency. Yet this is what is essential if the transformation is to be successful. And there is good news: If a school is successful in soliciting the wider constituency's support, the intraschool change effort becomes easier as well. There is a distinct reflexive—and even cumulative—affect.

For instance, shortly after Twomley arrived at MVA, one of the weaknesses of the school that it had to address right away was the physical plant situation. The buildings on campus were in sad shape and in need of a gigantic infusion of cash—a resource the school had little of. But it had to start somewhere. So it began by throwing away the trash and old equipment that had collected in buildings through the years.

By the time MVA had emptied the buildings, it had *filled 17 dumpsters.* It was incredible how much stuff had accumulated! It was also amazing the message this cleaning project began to send as the word got out: *Hey, we're serious here at MVA. We're really going to make a change. You can trust us—could you lend a hand?* This one act of "taking out the trash" helped spark a movement that led to a dramatic renewal in the campus's physical plant (something that I'll talk more about in chapter 18). The appropriate communication took place, setting a cumulative effect in motion, and people began giving their support at a crucial time in MVA's transformation . . . none of which would have happened if the reality of the good things happening had remained unknown!

So how do you get the good word out about the positive changes happening at your school and enlist widespread support among your constituency? There are three ways to do it: *communicate, communicate, and communicate some more.* Furthermore, such communication is of two kinds: verbal and nonverbal. Let's look at the latter first.

## Nonverbal Communication With Constituents

Leaders who have been at their particular school for any length of time often severely underestimate the power of nonverbal communication. But that can cost them dearly when they seek to garner support for making transformational changes. The antidote is to remember that when turning a school around, *everything communicates.* That pile of old desks in the hallway? It's telling every parent who visits your school that you like clutter in your hallways and quite possibly in your gradebook, too (whether you actually do or not is unfortunately irrelevant). That haphazardly organized mountain of books that you're trying to pass off as a library? It's informing students that books are for stacking rather than reading. And that flowerbed at the entrance to your school—the one that your science teacher just loves because of the vast variety of flora, fauna, and wildlife she can find in it? That's announcing to parents, "Don't send your children here—we can't care for our flowers, much less your kids." Ouch!

It is time that we quit making excuses about nonverbal communication and started accepting the reality that really, truly, unavoidably, everything communicates! And the only successful way to do so nonverbally with your constituents and enlist their support in turning around your school is to begin *systematically to offer the right message.* Are there desks in your hallway?

Burn them. Is the library a mess? Lock the door on the room until you get the books organized and usable. As for that flowerbed, have a weed-pulling party on Sunday morning at which you cook pancakes for everyone who shows up to help. And the list goes on and on.

Now, the great thing about nonverbal communication and your turn-around effort is that what can powerfully work against you can also be just as strongly in your favor once rectified. At SVA, for instance, the foyer in the ad building, while attractive in many ways, was terribly difficult to navigate for the uninitiated. Parents not familiar with the campus could walk in and have no real way of knowing where to go to get the information they needed. So early in the transformation effort the administration dramatically altered (with relatively little cash outlay) the rear center portion of the foyer—the place that your eye would naturally gravitate to. The school removed a glass wall, tossed the five-foot-tall counter, and in their place put a new, much smaller desk on top of a single, high-quality throw rug. The room was repainted brightly but tastefully, and a picture of Christ placed on the wall directly behind the desk. Immediately parents and other guests could now know precisely where to go to ask for help.

And here's the greater blessing: No one has to say a word to guests, yet every time they come into the ad building they "hear" "We care about your concerns, and we want to help you find the answers you're looking for." That's a great message for any school to send to its constituents.

So if you're looking to get the good word out about the great changes taking place in your school while trying to get constituents' support, never underestimate the power of nonverbal communication. Start with the most visible negative nonverbal communicator on your campus that you can fix, and then do it. Next, work your way down the list until as many of them as possible now communicate nonverbally in your school's favor. *Everything communicates*, and it's amazing what a little elbow grease and paint can do to speed the transformation of your school.

## Verbal Communication in Your Transformation Efforts

Now that we've looked at how nonverbal communication can work at your school, let's turn to verbal communication. While at times lacking the visceral "punch" of positive nonverbal communication, it nonetheless is crucial to helping spread the good word about your school and enlisting greater support among your constituents. This type of communication—whether done by the spoken or written word—needs to take place with at least five different groups of people: (1) staff members; (2) parents with students currently in your school; (3) alumni; (4) parents of prospective students for your school; and (5) upper-management school administrators (such as conference and union educational secretaries). Let's examine the type of communication required for each specific group.

1. *Staff members.* If you're a principal or administrator in a tanking school and you're attempting to return things to health again, you face a great temptation—particularly in smaller schools with few staff—to undercommunicate dramatically to staff members the vision for that brighter future. The faulty assumption is that once the principal, for instance, has stood and made his or her initial "rah! rah!" pitch for how things are going to turn around, that is sufficient to carry the school forward.

Nothing could be further from the truth. The reality is that you have to present the vision for change again and again and again to as many of the key figures in the school as possible—and especially to staff, as they are your frontline warriors in the battle to turn the school around. Change comes hard to even the brightest of us.

2. *Parents with students currently in your school.* For obvious reasons this group needs to have easy access to detailed information as to the great things that are happening or that are being attempted. Chances are that, if your school has been having very difficult times (even if you've been seeking to change that), many parents are sitting on the fence as to whether they will keep their students(s) enrolled for the future or not. So give them as many reasons as possible (as often as possible) for leaving their kids in your school.

Direct mailings can be effective here. If you don't already have one, start a monthly newsletter that you mail out. You could also have an e-mail list that any parent who wishes can join and get a weekly update on the school's progress. An occasional phone call from staff (or even trustworthy students, for that matter, depending on the nature of the information you're conveying) to all parents can go a long way toward defusing negative feelings about your institution. Also, quarterly town hall meetings at which parents can come to ask questions of the school administration are excellent venues for dispelling bad rumors and for sharing positive information. (If your school is conference- or union-sponsored, conduct the meetings in multiple locations throughout your region to ensure maximum participation from parents.) And there are other modes of communication as well.

In the end, what this type of communication with parents says is "I care about you. Your student is important to us, and we want to honor them and you." It also tells others, "We're serious about changing!" That kind of caring and information is indispensable in enlisting the support of your most important constituents: the ones already involved with your school.

3. *Alumni.* The next group of people that a school attempting to revitalize must make contact with is its alumni. At least two reasons demand it (and forgive me for my bluntness here): They have time, and they have money—two things that nearly every Adventist school needs desperately if it's trying to right its ship.

Perhaps it strikes you as crass that we contact alumni for the specific intent of tapping their chronological and financial resources. Certainly such requests of alumni can be done in inappropriate ways. But it is not inherently wrong to invite their support—far from it. In fact, many alumni—*if* they see that their alma mater is finally starting to make a sincere, concerted effort to return to vibrancy—would be disappointed *not* to be asked to participate in the rebuilding process.

For instance, let's consider the practice of contacting alumni for monetary support of school renewal efforts (chapter 18 will expand greatly on the very important topic of soliciting donors). We must first remember why anyone donates money at all: *People invest money to further their values in the world.* And assuming your alumni had a positive experience at your school when they attended it, it is only natural that, if possible, they want to contribute to its return to health so that the things they value might continue to be passed on to others.

But note carefully: Alumni will almost certainly not help with two types of appeals: (1) pleas to bail out a school that clearly does not have the needed leadership in place to return it to vibrancy; and (2) those they don't know about. So as long as you've done the preceding change steps with regard to school leadership correctly, be sure to communicate, communicate, communicate with your alumni!

Furthermore, don't be afraid to approach individual alumni with specific requests for your school. Tell them what you're trying to do and point out specifically what project you would like help with (appeals to put money into the "general fund" are rarely compelling). Then explain how they will potentially benefit from giving (seeing their values further propagated in the world, the pleasure of aiding students to get a great education, etc.). Finally, invite them to consider a specific dollar amount. In other words, don't say "Would you consider giving something?" but rather "Would you consider giving $5,000 to see this become a reality at our school?" Don't pressure them, but do ask them. If they need it, give them time to think over your request. And then see what the Lord does. You may be surprised how willing many alumni are to help return your school to health.* (Again, we'll explore this much more deeply in chapter 18.)

Of course, any willingness to assist at your school will depend largely on your level of communication. So consider including such individuals in your monthly mailings or weekly e-mail. If you don't have one already, develop an alumni association (this can bear positive results even for elementary schools). Or find some other way to transmit to them the good things going on at your school. However you do it, alumni can prove to be exceedingly valuable in turning a school in a positive direction.

4. *Parents of prospective students for your school.* This may seem so obvious as to be taken for granted. But if history is any indication, this group too often gets ignored.

For instance, Adventist families with school-age children that do *not* send their children to Adventist schools number in the thousands in this division. Many (if not most) know about Adventist education and are also aware of where the nearest Adventist school is. And many such parents would also choose to enroll their children in our schools if properly educated themselves as to the value of Adventist education—or how the terrible school they used to know (yours) is now the new, improving, turning around institution that their kids would thoroughly benefit from.

So how do you reach this segment of your constituency? Well, it's a little less straightforward than with the previous two groups. Disgruntled parents, for instance, rarely join registries that tell us who they all are. So sending a letter or an e-mail to them on a regular basis is probably going to be a hit-or-miss proposition. What to do?

*Hit the road!*

Sure, you need to do (if possible) mass mailings and so forth that trumpet to everyone in your constituency area what great things are now happening at your school. But few things convey positive information—and dispel long-held but now incorrect perceptions—about your school than you and/or your students showing up on their doorsteps. So do constituents' church services on Sabbath mornings. Divide up your staff and send them out to make presentations in as many of your constituent churches as possible. If you have them, send your choir, band, orchestra, basketball team, or any other important organization to do the same. Do whatever it takes to get live bodies in people's home territory and be available afterward for questions. Make sure that at each appointment you do more truth-telling: "You may have heard that our school has gone downhill. Well, it had, but I want you to know that we are better!" And then describe to them all the great changes being made to bring your school back to where it should be. Become a missionary for your school, generating buzz whenever you can.

And by the way: The closer to the action the person doing this truth-telling, the better. Principals are tops; teachers are next; and students—ones that are excited about what's going on at their school—can often meet or exceed the effectiveness of either principals or teachers. (Of course, combinations of the various groups are excellent, too.) Have people as intimately involved with the change efforts as possible to be your chosen emissaries. Their proximity will give credence to their message that others more distant from it will lack.

5. *Upper-management school administrators.* You need to keep education secretaries at the conference and union levels and their respective representatives abreast of what you're doing to reinvigorate your school. Call them often. Listen to their counsel. If appropriate, enlist them in the change process, such as by having them give encouraging talks to your board, having them present at constituency meetings, etc.

Several potential benefits can result from keeping your upper-management school administrators in the loop. First, they may have excellent ideas that they've gleaned from other portions of the NAD that have helped other schools turn around—ideas that you may not have access to unless you're in communication with administration. Second, knowing what you're doing at your school enables them to defend you better when those you upset locally call headquarters to complain (yes, this might even happen to you!). Third, though it's not something to count on, education secretaries at times have access to discretionary funds—resources much more likely to come your way if you've kept said secretary in the know regarding your school. And fourth, most education secretaries I have contact with are in their positions for a reason: They know education very well, and can thus provide a good sounding board for whatever ideas you throw out for helping your school.

Getting the good word out about what's changing at your institution and thus enlisting widespread support is crucial to successfully turning your situation around. Master this type of communication—both verbally and nonverbally—and good things will inevitably flow your direction.

---

* The General Conference has resources available to help nonprofits raise needed funds.

# CHAPTER 17

# Step 8:
# Embed the Positive Changes
# in the Culture of Your School

If you do the previous seven steps, good things are bound to happen at your school. A new day may well begin to dawn, and hope for the future may at last return. But how can you make the changes as close to permanent as possible?

This is crucial, because as we have already mentioned, schools that close don't do so overnight. Instead, it happens when well-intending people get lazy or distracted or ride on yesterday's triumphs. So, bottom line: Decline can return, even under good people's watch. But you can do some things to ensure as much as is possible a solid, healthy future for your school.

*1. Develop the best governing board that you can.* Here is perhaps one of the most overlooked areas of quality in a local school. But it's absolutely crucial to embedding the positive transformation taking place in its culture. The facts are that teachers, staff, and school administration all change over time. But generally your board has a much higher degree of consistent membership (or at least it should). Board member terms are usually staggered over various periods of time, allowing new members to benefit from previous members' wisdom and direction. Creating a strong board will thus establish a constant commitment to excellence in education that can exceed the tenure of any one gifted school administrator, regardless of his or her personal talent.

That said, it is true that most schools define board membership by local constitution as well as by the local union's educational code. Translation: The composition of your board may not be up to you. And since most constitutions and codes base board membership on geographical and/or demographic representation rather than competency, the challenge to build a great board can be formidable. Two suggestions, though, may be helpful.

First, do the best with what you have. If you can't alter the makeup of your board, you can still provide training for the members you currently have on how to function more efficiently as a board. That could include anything from basic skills (how to read a financial report)[1] to more complex ones (how to invest school funds or obtain loans for building projects). When possible, bring in the best minds you can to show your board how to think and act in terms of excellence.[2] And of course, your training should include a regular review of the school's vision and mission.

Second, if you have the option to adjust the composition of your board, consider sitting down with the person next in line above you (principal, education superintendent, etc.) and lay out your dream board. Perhaps it would include individuals known for their particularly deep spirituality and wisdom; their financial acumen; their ability to do effective project management; their experience with successful schools; and so on. Whatever the case, aim for excellence, and when the opportunity comes, make the request to invite the best-qualified people you can to join your board.

(One final reason that you need the strongest board possible if you're to embed positive changes in the culture of your school is this: The qualifications of your board may well determine how much money large donors are willing to give you. This is huge, and we'll talk about it more in chapter 18.)

*2. Pay special attention to the suggestions made earlier on having high-quality staff.* If you have, say, a weak new student registration *process* and then fix it, it will bear dividends for a while. But if you have weak *staff* and then either retrain them to a high standard or hire high-quality new staff, it will have positive results for years to come. Good people mean more to a school than good processes. Having high-quality staff that you treat well and can actually keep will go a long way toward incorporating the positive changes you're making into the culture of your school for years to come.

*3. Be very specific with local conference/union education officers as to your school's staffing needs and involve them intimately in hiring highly competent individuals.* "Aren't they already part of that process?" you might ask. Yes, they are. But often education secretaries, through no fault of their own, work in a bit of a vacuum. For instance, when it comes to hiring a new principal, school boards may put in a call to the office stating their need of such a person, but often leave out detailed information as to the specific *type* of principal required. Because the school board has not thought through their vision for their school, they have only a vague picture of whom they need to guide them to a better future. This can easily lead to simply hiring "the next résumé" and a continuation of a given school's decline.

But if you have a specific vision of the type of principal that your school demands (a destroyer captain versus a cruise ship captain, for instance) and can articulate what your school specifically needs, you're that much more likely to get a qualified leader at the helm. And note: *This will also bear dividends in the future, as the conference will now be that much more aware of what you're trying to do at your school.* And as things progress forward at it, they will likely take future specific staffing requests more seriously, thus helping to embed the positive changes for years to come.

*4. Establish trust funds/endowments to pay for specific, health-inducing programs.* True, this suggestion may not be open to all schools, as it does require a donor with significant amounts of money to make it possible. But if you have the resources available, this is an excellent path to follow. The idea is simple: Establish endowments that will support long-term programs at your school. Such funds might cover special advanced training for staff, exceptional academic programs for students (such as elite internships, field trip options, visiting lecturer series, and scholarships for exceptional students within specific disciplines), capital project endowments, endowments for student aid, and many other things.

I should point out that receiving moneys sufficient to establish meaningful endowments (that is, ones with enough principal to yield enough interest to do something significant with) is not easy. Few are the schools that have them, for endowments are usually the result of the happy marriage of two things: wealthy, generous alumni, and quality schools that exude excellence in all they do while showcasing consistent administrative acumen over time. Those two qualifications are pretty stiff! But if you have the option, pursue it.

*5. Alter administrative practices at the conference/union level.* This next statement may sound a little odd, but one of the "blessings" of having a system-wide decline in Adventist education is that we have multiple leadership groups that can contribute to turning things around (i.e., no one part of Adventism has to sit around and wait for someone else to do all the work). Schools, churches, and yes, the governing bodies found in our conference, unions, and so forth can all help revitalize our sagging educational fortunes.

Because of the weight that governing bodies carry in shaping Adventist education, I have dedicated chapter 19 to suggestions for how they can best use their influence.

## Here's the Point

The goal of each suggestion for embedding positive changes in your school is the development of long-term *momentum*. Proactively maintaining high standards with regard to the fundamentals of Adventist education and continually pursuing excellence in every category will help cement the health of your school. No, momentum can't eliminate all weaknesses from your educational program, nor can it guarantee that it won't face serious challenges in the future. But it can continually remind you *not to let those deficiencies and challenges remain unaddressed*—and that is of no small importance.[3] Positive momentum thus results from an attitude of excellence that you pursue continually until it becomes your automatic mode of operation. When this occurs, the positive changes brought about by earlier transformation efforts can become a firm part of the culture of your school.

---

[1] Never underestimate the financial inexperience of the average new board member. I speak from personal ignorance—er, experience. When I graduated from college and started pastoring and sitting on school boards, I didn't know a debit from a doughnut—and yet I was supposed to be a major player in the future of our children and their education! Basic training is thus key.

[2] Local conference or union education vice presidents often have good suggestions as to who can do such training, and may even be willing to help shoulder any expenses involved in bringing the expert to your school.

[3] After all, it may be that your school got into decline in the first place because someone who came before you ignored the need for developing positive momentum.

# CHAPTER 18

# The "Always Step"

There's a reason I do not call this "step 9." It is instead something that anyone who hopes to be successful in turning his or her school around will almost certainly have to execute continually. It is a step that ought to be in the forefront of school leaders' minds from the very beginning of the transformation effort, and if it is not, there is a great chance that the institution will not make the transformation successfully. And it is also the one that experienced administrators reading this book have been muttering to themselves, "When on earth are you going to get to that step, Anderson?" The "always step" is this: Always, always, always pursue genuine "transformational" money.

## But Isn't Pursuing Money Unspiritual?

Lest I be accused of going from a spiritual mode to a carnal one, let me quickly debunk one of the myths of money. The myth says this: "God will supply money to that which He blesses, and He will do so *automatically* without me lifting a finger." For our purposes, this myth also has a corollary that says, "If I and my school are just spiritual enough, we will have all the funds that we need."

Really?

It certainly is true that God will supply the necessary money to that which He blesses. And it's also true that we find examples in the Bible and in Adventist history of God's miraculously providing resources for His work "out of the blue." But those stories are the exception, not the rule. For while God will supply the dollars needed for His work, *He rarely, rarely does it without us actively pursuing it.*

The examples of God requiring leaders to seek funding for His work is long and (pardon the pun) rich: Moses called the Israelites to donate for the creation of the wilderness sanctuary (Ex. 35); King Joash urged the people to give liberally for the repair of the Solomonic Temple (2 Kings 12); the apostle Paul made appeals for donations to help God's people (1 Cor. 16); and Adventist history contains numerous stories of godly leaders asking church members (and others!) to give untold tens of thousands of dollars to further God's work in the world. In short, *God's leaders appropriately asking God's people for money to further His mission is standard operating procedure and thus a very spiritual thing to do.* In fact, *not* to ask for such money may actually be a sign of a *lack* of faith rather than an abundance of it.

So while it's true that greed and selfishness can easily worm their way into appeals for funds (and almost any other endeavor, for that matter), appropriately pursuing resources to enable your school to succeed is a very good thing and almost certainly essential to its successful transformation.

## Clarifying the Obvious

Now before someone mutters an emphatic "Duh, of course we need money!" the truth is that while most school leaders are always on the lookout for it, my experience is that very few of them seek anything *beyond operating capital.* They'll fight, push, and prod with their local board or a handful of donors to get adequate subsidy, additional operational funding, and the occasional capital improvement when needed. But their focus is on survival money rather than "transformational money."

"Transformational money" is the amount that it will realistically cost for your school to become a quality, attractive, and successful Seventh-day Adventist institution once again. Obviously, the amount needed will vary dramatically from school to school. A small elementary school may require less than $100,000, while a boarding academy or college may easily run into the millions. You should examine the following facets (at a minimum) of your school when determining how much transformational money you'll need:

*Physical plant:* What will it take to make it safe, accessible, and inviting? (Note: The answer may be "Construct a new building—and possibly somewhere else!")

*Teaching/staff resources:* What supplies, advanced training, additional positions, etc., does your school need to be an excellent one?

*Extracurricular activities*: What activities, advanced spiritual training opportunities, AP-type classes, regular field trips, music training options, and so forth will set your school apart from others in the area as a top-notch education choice for parents to choose for their students?

And there may be other areas to study as well.

Once you have established a reliable figure that indicates how much transformational money you'll need, the following 10 steps may help you obtain it.

1. *Fix the three laws of transformational school finance firmly in mind:*

*Law 1*: "If all I seek is money for operations, my school will never turn around."

*Law 2*: "Money is a secondary indicator—that is, a lack of money is nearly always the result of a lack of quality and/or vision in my school, not an absence of people who will donate money to it." (Corollary: "Money follows value and vision regularly, but it rarely precedes them.")

*Law 3*: "I will receive transformational money for my school only if I devote major portions of my time to securing it."

2. *Put as many of the eight steps mentioned in the preceding chapters as possible into action.*

To reiterate what I said in chapter 16, remember why people—be they institutions or individuals—will give money to your school: *to make an investment that will further their values in the world.* This necessarily narrows the field of possible donors, as your school already has a set of values (as discussed earlier) that it needs to run by. However, those potential donors that do reflect your school's values will be far more inclined to give you substantial amounts of transformational money if you can first demonstrate that you are actively implementing those mutually shared goals.

3. *If possible, find someone else to take care of procuring operational funds.*

If you're *the* leader of a school, you must free yourself up to pursue transformational dollars. It is a time-consuming process, and the complexities of finding mere operational funding, while certainly requiring attention, do not necessarily demand *your* attention (obviously, only you know how much you should involve yourself here, so use your judgment).

So if at all possible, find someone qualified to take care of procuring and overseeing operational funds. In larger schools this may be easier than in smaller ones. However, even one-room elementary schools often have local church members nearby that may have the necessary skill to help you and the time to volunteer, freeing up your time to seek transformational funds actively.

4. *Identify potential donors of transformational money.*

Think carefully: Whom do you know—or whom does someone else that you know know—that has both sufficient funds and sufficiently shared values with your school that they could be potential partners in obtaining transformational money? True, depending on your type of school, the answer to this question may be limited to "the general congregations of my constituent churches." But more often than not, there are also specific individuals (or organizations) that the Lord has blessed with substantial financial resources that you could invite to partner with your school. Pray, ask around for help, and then make a list of potential donors.

The next two steps overlap so much that it's difficult to separate them. So I'll state them together:

5. *Make the request for transformational funds from your potential donors.*

6. *Generate short-term wins and capitalize on them as soon as possible.*

Perhaps an illustration from Mount Vernon Academy will help explain their inseparable nature.

When the MVA turnaround began, two areas requiring much attention were the boys' and girls' dormitories. The obvious problem, though, was the same monotonous refrain echoed by academies across the country: "We have no money." So what to do?

Actually, it was not that they didn't have *any* money, for Twomley had already done some vision casting about what MVA could become, and made some requests to donors. His work produced about $125,000 toward renovating the dorms. But as helpful as that was, it was still far less than what the school needed to complete the project. In fact, the donated money was enough only to remodel one dorm room and the dean's living quarters in the girls' dorm— hardly the stuff that constitute entire physical plant renovations.

Or was it?

As it turned out, Twomley was well aware of the importance of generating short-term wins and then capitalizing on them. The one dorm room and the dean's apartment began to be remodeled—and the effect of having something like that actually happening on MVA's dilapidated campus was electrifying. *Imagine,* constituents thought, *the girls' dorm at MVA—just one of a campus full of buildings so antiquated and outmoded that the school had to fill 17 dumpsters with trash to begin any remodeling—was now actually having some genuine progress made in it. Incredible! Who would've thought it could happen?*

But simply generating happy thoughts for MVA was not the school's sole goal. Principal Twomley quickly used this good press to ask for more transformational money, and indeed, more money arrived—even before the work crew had finished the one dorm room and the dean's apartment! Soon the academy had sufficient dollars—all $1.5 million of them—to remodel the girls' dorm completely. And as progress continued on it, the school requested additional money, and it poured in for the *guys'* dorm until *it* was completely remodeled. All this at MVA—the school that just a few short months earlier trembled on the verge of closure.

This snippet from MVA's history should underline in bold letters the necessary unity of steps 5 and 6 in raising transformational money. The process of asking for funds, using them to generate short-term wins for your school, then requesting more funds, creating more short-term wins, seeking more funds, and so forth, is a sound one, and is one that we should not underestimate in its importance. *Wise and godly donors—particularly those with great wealth—will rarely simply hand over their money to a school that cannot first demonstrate that they know what to do with it.* Generating short-term wins says to these and all donors, "Your investment is safe with us"—a priceless message for schools looking for transformational money.

A final note on step 5 specifically may be helpful. As mentioned in chapter 16, when asking potential donors to give your school transformational funds, it is crucial to tell them *what* it is you're requesting ("We need $65,000 for the new student center," for instance), *why* you're asking for it ("We believe a new student center will provide a much-needed haven for student life, spiritual programming, the building of school spirit, and safe socializing in an easily supervised setting") and the potential benefits that you envision for both your school *and* the donor if they choose to contribute funds. ("The new student center will send a much-needed message to students and parents alike that we care about them. It will boost long-term campus morale and spirituality because of the nature of programming that we will have there. Named in your honor, it will stand as a constant testament to the fact that the students' spiritual and social decisions are very important to us and to God, and that we want to give them the best possible footing in this regard.") You will also probably need to tell them who your leadership team is: yourself, your staff, and your board (more on this below). Such specificity—given both verbally and usually in writing—will help potential donors see that you have a well-thought-out plan for the revitalization of your campus, and thus for how you will employ their funds. It can go a long way toward helping them decide to donate to the cause.

7. *Keep donors regularly informed of how you are using their funds, progress on the project, etc.*

One error that people new to raising money make is to simply take the money and run. They're so thrilled that someone actually gave their school some money that they dive right into the project after barely saying "Thanks!" Some may even consider it "unspiritual" to keep donors informed, since "they gave it to God's work, and they should trust that it'll be used appropriately without having to know where every cent went."* Unfortunately, there are few better ways to ensure that a donor will never donate again! People want and deserve to know what's happening with their gift to your school. Keep them in the loop regularly through the medium of their choice (phone, e-mail, etc.).

Regular communication is also crucial in case you need to request more money for a particular project from someone who's already donated to it. It's much easier to go back and ask for additional funds from someone that you updated on the project just a week before than it is to pop up after a year of silence and say, "Wow, remember me? I need more of your money!" Some donors are pleased to be able to give until a project's completed, even if that means they have to pay more than first anticipated (and obviously, you need to strive to be realistic in your initial cost projections!). Keeping them up-to-date will help them see that you're serious about what you're doing and that you can be trusted to follow through appropriately.

8. *Follow the suggestions in chapter 16 for getting the good word out about your successes.*

Godly people of substantial means with sympathies for your school must be good stewards of the money that the Lord has given to them. The more they hear about the transformation taking place on your campus, the more they can legitimately say, "I like and trust what they're doing at that school. I will give from my resources to continue its transformation."

9. *Develop an outstanding governing board.*

We said quite a bit in chapter 17 about how to use one to embed positive changes in the culture of your school. But now we must look at how a strong board can help you secure transformational money.

As mentioned in step 7, potential donors—particularly ones with considerable wealth—will probably need to know who your school's leadership is. Obviously that includes the principal, school presidents (at colleges and universities) or head teacher. But it also involves any other key leaders that will have a role in stewarding transformational money, particularly your governing board.

Now, granted, not every potential donor requests such information. But for those who do, their reason for asking should be obvious. As mentioned previously, boards can have a tremendous influence on the overall long-term direction and quality of your school. Can those considering donating substantial funds to your school trust that their gift will indeed do what they intend for it over the long haul—even if school administration changes? Only a solid board can come close to guaranteeing this, and the development of an *outstanding* board can provide great incentive for potential donors to give transformational dollars.

10. *Continually communicate your vision for the school.*

There is no substitute for this. Keep the vision before your constituents. And do so whether you're asking them for money at the time or not. Vision casting is a transformational fund-raiser's stock-in-trade, a key that can unlock the hopes and dreams of generations to come. "Where there is no vision, the people perish" the Bible says (Prov. 29:18, KJV). But *with* vision, your school—including its transformational coffers—can thrive once again.

In detailing each of these 10 steps, my hope is that the overall message of this "always step" is clear: *If all you're looking for is money to tide you through the next school year (or perhaps just the next week), that's likely to be all you'll get.* And the tragedy is that many good school leaders fall prey to a survival mentality that limits their ability to turn a school around. Don't let it happen to you! Thus, don't merely aim for getting operating expense money, but instead always pursue genuine transformational money.

---

\* And yes, I've heard this from an actual leader's lips.

# CHAPTER 19

# The Role of Conference/ Union/Division Administration in the Revitalization Process

In the preface I talked about my "foolishness" in taking on a task that involves a profession that I have never worked in. Now I will move from foolishness to unmitigated insanity and discuss administration, another area in which, yes, I have never been personally involved. (But this is nearing the end of the book. If you're still reading by now, a little insanity may prove refreshing.)

Kidding aside, there are at least four broad categories in which church administrators who want to revive Adventist education might be helpful: realism versus optimism, problem-specific competency, leadership development, and accountability.

## Realism Versus Optimism

Contrary to the popular stereotype that many in my generation have, nearly all of the conference, union, and division leaders that I've met are genuinely good people. They are a sincere and most helpful group of professionals, and I have appreciated the vast majority of my interactions with them over the past 14 years.

However, there is a suggestion that I would offer that may be of assistance in turning Adventist education around: When speaking about the state of Adventist education—whether privately or publicly—favor realism over unjustified optimism. If things are truly going wonderfully, say so. And yes, if things are collapsing, be realistic and paint an honest picture so that employees, constituents, and anyone else might know what's really going on.

In my experience many church administrators are reluctant to admit that our education system is in dire straits. And even if they do refer to problems publicly, they too often quickly follow with "but let's look at the positive things that are happening with our schools," and the problems soon get drowned out by a chronicling of random events scattered around the conference/union/division—events hardly related enough to warrant such optimistic talk.

The temptation to downplay bad educational news is understandable. Presidents, union secretaries, treasurers, and other administrators often find themselves under tremendous pressure to produce good results—pressure both from their immediate supervisors and, of course, their constituents. And it takes immense courage simply to stand up and give a realistic public picture of our educational system.

But I would suggest that *the Adventist educational system desperately needs high-level church administrators who regularly and publicly acknowledge the real extent of our education woes and what it will realistically take to fix them—and then pursue those solutions even if it costs them favor with others.*

The reason is simple: How can division-wide transformation take place otherwise? I still vividly remember reading the final report from a union constituency session that briefly mentioned the dire situation of education in its territory (and it was dire!), followed by a single-sentence vow to research the problem and try to find solutions. *That's it?* I thought. *One sentence? This is our solution to a denominational problem so severe that it could cripple our witness in the world within a generation or two?*

To be fair, some talks and articles in church publications have occasionally presented realistic pictures of education in the North American Division. But their numbers demand a boost. And while the effort for educational health must ultimately take place at the local level, I respectfully suggest that we desperately need church administrators at all levels—particularly conference and union presidents—in this division who will make educational resurrection a top *and public* priority. Only then can we overcome the institutional inertia to accomplish the wholesale changes required; only then might it be possible to grab the attention of a wide swath of the NAD's active membership and enlist them in the rebuilding process.

I believe that our schools are the legs that ultimately keep the Advent movement running. Without our schools being in working order, our effectiveness in our portion of the world will continue to suffer. It's time to be optimistic when circumstances warrant it, and the rest of the time to be regularly, publicly realistic about both our problems and their potential fixes.

## Problem-specific Competency

One of the hardest things to do in the crisis environment that is Adventist education is the thing that needs doing the most: End the crisis! There are perhaps many reasons for that, but one of the top ones is this: Simply running the "educational ship" when it's in *good* shape already takes all of one's time, leaving nothing left over to deal with "extras" (such as, for instance, keeping the ship from sinking). It's like the band that played on even while the *Titanic* slid under the waves. "No hope of saving the ship, so we might as well continue doing what we were originally hired to do."

Here's where I have great sympathy with my administrative associates, for I know firsthand how extraordinarily difficult it can be to return an organization to health when just the day-to-day duties alone are enough to choke an entire team of draft horses. The local church illustrates this in my own sphere. For instance, in a given congregation it might have been years since someone from "the outside" (i.e., not a member's child) has been baptized, or perhaps the church has some chronic, serious issues that must be dealt with before it can grow again. But for too many members, these facts pale in importance when compared with the church's "need" to have the pastor chair committees, direct boards, answer mail (both snail and e), write for the newsletter, fund-raise for building projects, and generally keep the existing church machinery running. So pastors find themselves constantly challenged: Do I address the politically important, but of possibly little eternal value, task of the moment? Or do I try to solve the church's core issues, so that we might not merely keep the doors open but actually thrive again in the future? It is at times an agonizing decision to make.

And there's only one right answer: Do both.

Here's the truth about being a pastor, a teacher, and yes, a church administrator in these troubled last days in the Adventist Church: We have got to find ways to accomplish both of these things. This truth is harsh, cruel, merciless—but it is nonetheless true. For the pastor, it means training others to take on as many of the day-to-day tasks of church life as soon as possible so that he or she can focus as much time as possible on solving the potentially life-threatening problems facing the church and move it into health. For the administrator, it may mean the same: Put first things first. Work hard to give the individuals you supervise as much responsibility for the "standard" parts of your job as you can, and then increasingly spend your time tackling the bigger issues.

Here's the reason I spend time analyzing the busyness of church administrators—and I must tell you in advance that I mean no disrespect by what follows: *Almost every time I've asked a church administrator—be they president, vice president, treasurer, education vice president, whatever, in conferences and unions across the country—what they believe will move our education system back into health, the answer I've received is . . . a long pause, followed by great uncertainty.*

Please don't misunderstand me here. Such men and women are not idiots, nor are they incompetent in carrying out the basic requirements of their jobs. Far from it! They are instead (in my experience) overworked, and some are gifted, not in the area of leadership, but rather in that of management. Often they are so overwhelmed with keeping up with the day-to-day functioning of their respective offices that they just don't have the time to deal with the pressing but very complex and life-threatening problems that Adventist education faces.

But however understandable their predicament may be, the reality still remains: We are in desperate need of *problem-specific competency—that is, administrators who are not only competent in the day-to-day tasks of their job, but who are also skilled in facing successfully the problems that plague Adventist education.* I respectfully submit that we must have administrators who can come to the table of any of our troubled schools with a reasonable understanding of what it requires to meet the needs of that school not merely for the moment but for the long haul.

Such competency is available. We have some highly gifted church administrators in this division who have much to share with those less endowed. Additionally, we have a handful of principals with proven track records of taking schools in terrible shape and bringing them back into vibrancy. In short, while we may not know all the answers to every problem that Adventist education faces, there are resources available that, if properly tapped, could help schools across the division.

I would respectfully submit that administrations at the various levels of our church ask some key questions. In the case of our struggling schools, do we know how to turn them around? If the answer is no, how will we discover and implement the correct solutions?

These seem to me to be reasonable yet essential questions to tackle if we are to find systemic solutions to our educational problems. The potential for eternal loss if our schools continue to decline is such that we can no longer afford to have "the band play on" any longer. We need problem-specific competency so that our schools can get the counsel and the mentoring they must have to move out of crisis mode and into life once again. An administrator's task may well be, then, to free up enough time either to become problem-specifically competent or to maintain competence in this crucial area.

And one final note. Conference and union presidents carry an immense amount of authority in the NAD—far more than the education vice presidents who work under them. If there's an education vice president who really knows his or her stuff when it comes to educational reform, and they are working for a conference or union president who for whatever reason does not fully support that education vice president, it will seriously diminish the ability of the latter to do his or her job. While it is true that there may be reasons to "rein in" an overly ambitious education vice president, I can't think of too many valid ones, particularly when such individuals know what they're doing. Our conference and union presidents are truly the gatekeepers when it comes to widespread educational reform in the Adventist Church, and thus my plea is simple: Either lead the charge for it yourself, presidents, casting the vision while allowing your education vice president do the legwork; or equip *them* with broad authority to accomplish what has to be done—particularly when it comes to their authority on the boards of our schools.

## Leadership Development

This one is hugely important, so much so that our success here will make or break us in our quest to return our schools to health. It begins with an essential question that I wish all church administrators could ask themselves: What are we currently doing to recruit and develop spiritually minded, transformational, visionary leaders *specifically for the role of school principal?* As we've noted, such individuals are currently rare birds. Yet having the right kind of leader in our schools today is absolutely essential if we are to restore them to health. Such a transformation simply cannot take place without solid leadership.

In chapter 12 I discussed briefly how we need to address this dearth of leadership not only locally but division-wide if it's to be effectively rectified.

So let's see if we can take a stab at what a possible solution might look like.

As mentioned in chapter 12, few people currently clamor for the job of principal. The church administrator's challenge, therefore, is not simply to train people to *be* effective principals, but to help them *want* to be trained *and* to be willing to meet the requirements necessary to become one. Here are some suggestions for achieving that end.

1. *Revive the concept of "calling."* The practical among us may chafe a bit at this suggestion topping my list of how to recruit competent leaders. It may appear to be an overly "spiritual" answer to a very nuts-and-bolts problem. But I put it in first place because of the reality of principal-hood today: The job is incredibly taxing, and only someone who is a fool, a controlling egomaniac, or a leader called by God is likely to accept it—and frankly, I'd like to see us narrow the field to include only the last category! A revival of the concept of calling can be a great help in this direction.

A parallel from the ministerial world may be helpful. When I was in eighth grade, my homeroom teacher, Marc Lovejoy, told me after hearing me give a talk for speech class, "You should be a preacher!" I was appalled. Being a preacher when I grew up was not last on my list of things to do in life— it was *after* whatever was last. The idea of dedicating my life to the ministry stood in diametric opposition to what I knew I wanted to do (go to Detroit and work for one of the big three automakers designing cars as an engineer). And there was absolutely no way I was going to get myself roped into being a pastor for the rest of my days.

As you may have noticed, I am now a pastor.

How did that happen? The only reason I gave up my dreams and entered the ministry is that *God called me to do so*. It's a lengthy story as to how that happened, and I won't go into it now. But the bottom line is that God made it abundantly clear to me that I was to change my major in college from engineering to theology. At the time I hated the idea. I kicked, screamed, and ranted, and I barely got to like it well enough by my senior year of college even to get a job. But today I now see why God summoned me to the ministry. I can honestly say that I'm very, very honored to be where I am . . . *and yet no amount of money would be enough to entice me to be a pastor*. Don't misunderstand. There's a great deal to rejoice in when you're a pastor. And make no mistake: Being an effective pastor today is incredibly difficult—much like being an effective principal. And consequently, I am convinced that there is simply no way to adequately "incentivise" the role of the principal (or pastor!) to meet our current need *without* a revival of the concept of calling.

So if you're a church administrator, what might be some ways that you could help restore the concept of the Lord leading someone to do a certain work, including being a principal? Undoubtedly it begins (and continues) with prayer. There is no substitute for this. Next, you could utilize each of the forms of communication available to your office. Write about God's calling of His people in the newsletters you send out. Print up bulletin inserts on the topic for the churches you serve. For those of you who preach in local churches on occasion, talk about it in your sermons. And those of you who have administrative duties involving secondary or college education, ask to take occasional chapels, colloquiums, education club meetings, or business club meetings, and challenge the students to think and pray about what God would like them to do with their lives—and might it be to work as a principal?

In all of these modes of communication I would strongly recommend presenting the post of principal as what it is: missionary work of the highest order, requiring the most dedicated, skilled, and effective (and brave?) individuals the denomination has to offer. Point out that no more influential post exists in the entire Adventist educational system than that of principal—that it is a job with the potential of helping generations of students become citizens of heaven and good citizens of earth until then. (And yes, I do think it's important to be that specific—that is, to urge students to consider being a *principal* instead of simply "pursuing a career in Adventist education." We are in a crisis, and rather than promoting just the general idea of a career in education we must make specific calls for a specific position that we badly need filled with high-quality people.) Sure, some students, for instance, will scoff: "Me, a principal? Yeah, right!" But some may be sitting there, under the influence of the Holy Spirit, waiting for someone to actualize what God has been preparing them for all along. Make the call to the students, and be specific. God knows what He's doing and whom He needs, and the work is much more likely to get done if we do our part and present the invitation.

A final point: Could it be that one of the reasons that people feel a low sense of God's specific calling to being a principal is that we ourselves—that is, those of us on boards or in church administration that search for and hire school staff—have come to see Adventist education as a purely professional entity rather than a primarily spiritual one? In other words, maybe it's not just that our members or the students in our colleges don't think in terms of being "called" by God to be a principal—but maybe we don't either! Could it be that when searching for a principal, we look *first* at an applicant's administrative talents or their problem-solving abilities or their leadership skills or whatever and no longer ask *first* that most fundamental of questions: Do you feel that the Lord has called you to this position? If the person's answer is yes, *then* we can (and should) examine the other questions of skills, for they are important in confirming that we have the right individual. But if the answer is no or "Huh?" or "What does that have to do with me taking this position?" we are interviewing the wrong person for the job! *God is still in charge of His work. He knows who is needed when, where, and for how long, and He still calls the shots as He sees fit—and it all works wonderfully if we are listening to His direction.*

*2. Financially reward the principal's role.* No, this is not contradicting point 1! Rather, it is simply following the biblical principle that "a worker is worth his keep." A principal's job is, generally speaking, harder than a teacher's, and I suggest that it's time that the salary reflect that fact. Currently, the pay difference between teaching and principaling at the secondary level, for instance, is only a few thousand dollars a year—barely enough to cover the costs of the Excedrin and therapy needed to survive the job. Should we not instead make it clear not only spiritually, but also financially, that great things are at stake when a person takes on the task of principal? And would it not further convey to potential principals that conference, union, and division administrations are dead serious in their calls for top-notch school leaders if we were to boost commensurately the salary for that pivotal job?

I am familiar with the objections to this suggestion. The most common seems to be that if we up the salary, people will clamor for the job just to get the extra money. And truth be told, if we did increase the salaries for the position, some would indeed try to become principals just for that reason. That is a problem that we would need to address. (Although, given the climate in the principaling field today, the job just might be self-regulating in this regard. That is to say, if someone became a principal of an academy just for the extra money, it is possible that they would quit at or before the end of their first year as the magnitude of the responsibility they had lightly taken on sunk in!) However, I don't foresee it being a major obstacle. The pay raise I would suggest is only to compensate principals more fairly for what's required of them, not to make them fabulously wealthy.

This brings up the obvious question: How much should we raise the salary beyond the maximum teacher salary? Obviously, a uniform number for each situation in the NAD would be difficult to generate, and I don't possess the expertise to speculate on a workable formula. But in my estimation, whatever the pay increase would be, it should say clearly to the principal: "We understand the enormity of the task that we've given you, and we value your high performance under such pressure."

Again, not all will agree with this notion. But I still believe the idea of increased remuneration for principals is one whose time has come. Church administration has declared in the past how valuable Adventist education is. Shouldn't our pay scale reflect the sentiment?[1]

*3. Develop internship programs for principals.* To unwrap this idea, let's take a look at a portion of the Adventist *ministerial* career track. The idea of being an intern is well ingrained in the Adventist pastoral system. Upon graduating with a degree in theology, every student knows that there's a good chance they'll get assigned as an intern to a successful church in the particular conference that hired them. They could be there for anywhere from one to four years, and then the conference will place them in a congregation or congregations of their own. After some time has passed, the pastor leaves to get his or her master's degree, and then returns again to the field.[2] In this way, the church has a reasonable expectation that theology graduates who heretofore have had primarily theoretical training in their field will now gain basic pastoral and leadership skills.

Could we not set up the same type of process for potential principals?

Various attempts have sought to get this very thing started in various parts of the division. But thus far, either because of lack of funds or lack of interest from colleges or administrators, none have flown very high or very long. Yet the concept is sound: Take potential principals that show promise for the task and match them with experienced, successful principals somewhere in the NAD. Let them work together as principal and vice principal for one to four years, then send the "intern" off to lead a school of their own in a different locale. Later, sponsor them to get their master's in administration (or another master's degree, where appropriate), and then return them again to a school. In this way the success of one principal can become the success of many, and our schools will be that much more likely to return to health.

Certainly there are numerous obstacles to implementing such a plan, not the least of which is changing the mind-set of education majors to include a bit more moving around the country than they had anticipated on their way to becoming full-fledged principals. But this does not seem insurmountable, particularly if our Adventist administrative system would make it mandatory to do so. (Heresy? Perhaps. More on this in the next section, on accountability.)

However we do it, there remains a desperate need for qualified principals in our division. *I cannot conceive of a successful system for filling this need that does not include matching inexperienced principals-to-be with proven, battle-tested professionals that have track records of leading healthy schools.* And in my foolish but passionately held opinion, continuing on with the division-wide principal training system we have (none) is a recipe for continuing to get the results that we're currently getting. (See chapter 8.)

All three suggestions—reviving the notion of being called by God, raising the salaries of principals, and developing internship programs—cannot be accomplished at the local level. They require specific intervention from church administrators. I unabashedly plead with our administrators: Will you give the concepts your support in tangible, actionable ways?

## Accountability

It is a sad reality that the word "accountability" has become almost exclusively a negative one in our culture. Each of us wants to be free, and who would dare to tell us what to do? It is the spirit of the age, one of postmodern relativistic thinking that says that all ideas and behaviors are of equal value and that only an ignorant, intellectual dwarf would conclude otherwise.

Where are my fellow dwarves? And might we elect some of them to administration in our church—a church that I believe has lost much of its effective witness in the world because we no longer hold one another accountable?

I need to be careful here, for this section will be easy to misunderstand. So let me be clear what I mean when I call for church administrators to bring more accountability into Adventist education.

I do *not* mean that we should usher in oppressive big brother-ism that encourages conference, union, and other church officers to be obsessed with accountability for its own sake rather than for the cause of Christ. Nor do I suggest that we should implement accountability to the point of micro-management, in which church administration seeks to keep a finger in every pot for the sake of absolute control. And no, I do not think we should implement accountability for the kind of criteria that can be met 100 percent . . . and yet have some employees and institutions be as spiritually dead on the inside as the devil himself.[3] This is *not* what I'm talking about when I speak of accountability.

Instead, I simply mean that we need (1) to have excellent education policies; and that if we have them, we need (2) to enforce them properly.

A couple of questions may help shed light on this concept, though I readily admit that they can be unpleasant to ask and answer honestly: How many of our conferences or unions have policies on the books that state that each church will be a constituent of a local church school—even if they don't have a church school on their property or even children attending any church school? (Answer: Many.) How many conferences or unions currently attempt to enforce this? What about pastors that openly oppose Adventist education? Do we appropriately hold them accountable for their actions—particularly when their ordination was a recognition of their agreement to uphold church standards, outreach, and mission? What about pastors that do nothing about Adventist education, the ones who help kill our schools through neglect? Is there anything being done about such conduct, to redirect such pastors kindly but firmly into better ways of supporting the Adventist mission? And what about regular teacher and principal evaluations? Are they happening in our schools? If not, how do we expect to achieve and/or maintain a high degree of excellence? And what about both teacher and principal contracts? Because of the frequent lack of regular evaluations, could it be that such documents have lost their effectiveness in that, on the one hand, teachers can decry the lack of security they provide from year to year, while on the other hand a teacher can be grossly incompetent in a variety of areas and still be contractually protected from appropriate administrative intervention?

Perhaps most important of all is the need for *vision* accountability. This has nothing to do with optometry, but everything to do with what the concept of a successful future that leadership should have for their particular school. If ever there was a need for accountability in our schools, surely this is it! The denomination should assist principals and other school leaders in developing a preferred and compelling grasp of what their school should become. They need to be helped in developing specific benchmarks that will demonstrate success in moving toward that vision. And then, yes, the local conference, union, or other administrative body must appropriately hold the administration of a local school accountable for meeting those benchmarks.

Again, I am not trying to throw stones here. I have too much respect for our church and its leadership to do so! But I nonetheless feel that the questions and observations in the previous two paragraphs reveal serious flaws in how we conduct ourselves when it comes to accountability in our educational system. I fear that we have become too much a part of the surrounding culture, imbibing its impulses and ways of "doing business," including that of little accountability. Surely, together, we can do better.

In my understanding, to implement a healthy state of accountability for our schools requires at least three things, none of which are rocket science, but all of which are indispensable.

First, proper accountability requires *a recasting of the vision for Adventist education*. This is crucial! Accountability without vision is only a few steps removed from slavery. But accountability with a clearly articulated grasp of what a blessing it is to have Adventist education fully functioning, thriving, and producing loving and lovable Christians who will help finish Christ's work—there's no substitute for that! So communicate the vision of what healthy Adventist schools can be like. Enlist the interest and yes, passion, of your employees (pastors, teachers, staff) and constituents. Show them a future that is bright with vibrant graduates doing their Master's bidding well and effectively. Restoking this fire may require time, and a number of conference or union pastors'/teachers'/principals' meetings may need to take place before the vision can begin to take hold. But it must be cast *first*, so that church employees and constituents alike may have ample time to grasp that vision for themselves.

Second, we must *articulate clear guidelines for the kind of behavior that will achieve the vision*. For instance, have pastors articulate their plans in writing for helping their churches support Adventist education each year. Be clear that the schools themselves will conduct teacher and staff evaluations each year with no exceptions. And have/help principals of schools that are in dire straits develop a detailed plan, on paper, for reversing the trends at their school.

Finally, *hold employees and constituents accountable for the clearly articulated behavioral guidelines.* Again, this is not rocket science, but it does work. If you ask an employee to carry out a clearly outlined task that they've agreed to do, it is entirely reasonable to expect them to perform it. And if they don't, they need reminding, retraining, or possibly removal from their position. God's money and mission are too valuable to spend resources on providing a gravy train for employees who do not take those things seriously.

So again, a challenge for our church administrators: In your sphere of influence, is there a compelling vision being cast for Adventist education? Are there reasonable behavioral guidelines that have been clearly articulated to your employees and constituents that will help attain such a vision? Are you holding people appropriately accountable for those behavioral guidelines? If the answer to any of these questions is no, then I would respectfully suggest that we have some important work to do if Adventist education is to thrive again.

These four categories—realism versus optimism, problem-specific competency, leadership development, and accountability—are fertile areas within which church administration can help turn Adventist education around. God is looking for leaders in the upper levels of our church's management structure who can interpret our troubled times correctly and make changes that will help revive our schools. May God grant them the courage and wisdom necessary to do so swiftly and effectively.

---

[1] I realize in making this suggestion that our current pay scale requires extensive effort to alter, i.e., local conferences and unions are not at liberty to change it at will. Who will be the first to suggest this change at appropriate levels, then, that it might indeed be changed?

[2] Alternately, conferences will at times send a freshly graduated theology major straight to seminary to receive their master's, which would be followed by an internship at a local church.

[3] In days past pastors' monthly reports asked, "How many pieces of literature did you pass out this month?" and other such minutia, reportedly leading some pastors to give 15 pieces of literature away faithfully each month . . . to their wives and children.

# CHAPTER 20

# Let Us
# Become Normal

In the previous 19 chapters we've covered a lot of ground. We've dissected the causes of Adventist educational decline (both imagined and real); we've seen how not to turn around a dying school ("Keep doing what we're doing!"); and we've taken a look at an eight-step (plus one "always step") strategy for how to restore it to vibrancy once again.

One remaining thing still demands our attention. It's something that goes beyond any one administrator or local school leader to the heart of every believing Seventh-day Adventist Christian, whether directly involved with an educational institution or not. In fact, it's a matter so crucial that if we neglect it, no amount of sweat, technique, or savvy will make up for it; a matter so pivotal that it will determine not merely the success of our school system, but of our church—or more to the point, of our prophetic movement.

This most pressing of matters is . . . *revival.*

Ellen White had this to say about the topic: "A revival of true godliness among us is the greatest and most urgent of all our needs. *To seek this should be our first work.* There must be earnest effort to obtain the blessing of the Lord, not because God is not willing to bestow His blessing upon us, but because we are unprepared to receive it. . . . But it is our work, by confession, humiliation [humility], repentance, and earnest prayer, to fulfill the conditions upon which God has promised to grant us His blessing. A revival need be expected only in answer to prayer."[1]

That's what ails us the most, the problem that no amount of cunning or finesse can compensate for. For at the end of the day Adventist families, Adventist churches, and yes, Adventist schools are all first and foremost *spiritual* entities requiring *spiritual* discernment to be of maximum *spiritual* benefit to God and the world around them.

*Now, hold on a moment!* some of you might be thinking. *You've just spent a chunk of time detailing a slew of practical, hands-on guidelines for turning around a declining Adventist school. Are you now suggesting that those things aren't important—that we should "just pray" and "be spiritual" and everything will be all right?*

I need to be careful here, for a misunderstanding could be costly. I wholeheartedly believe in the practical action steps that I've outlined in the preceding chapters. They are crucial and in most cases indispensable to transforming a school! And *every one of those practical action steps ought to be performed against the backdrop of revival, for this is our core deficiency, both personally and corporately.* We have not simply lost our love of a few Adventist education fundamentals—we have too often lost our first love of Jesus! And if we are to turn ourselves and our school system in the NAD around, we must regain it. Yes, we must passionately pursue enrollment fixes and financial fixes in our schools. But we are to be driven *primarily* not by dollars and enrollment figures or any other empirical tally, but by the Holy Spirit of God. In fact, *do we even dare to imagine that somehow we, using our otherwise valid and carefully executed practical steps alone, could concoct a successful school transformation* without *a revival of true godliness taking place in our students and staff and boards?* I pray not. As important as financial solvency and enrollment stats are, not a single school will be "successful" in these areas without having their front-and-center goal being first to know Jesus Christ and to bring glory to Him!

So what are we to do? How are we to obtain revival? How can we as individuals and institutions experience this vital union with Christ, becoming obedient to His will and joyful in His presence? There is to be no mystery regarding this. Here are the steps that history, the Word of God, and the writing of Ellen G. White have shown us.

1. *Become a person of prayer.* "A revival need be expected only in answer to prayer," the prophet said. It means that no further steps are possible till this one has taken place. The Bible tells us to "pray continually" (1 Thess. 5:17). This is the case for many reasons, but the biggest one may be: "The first lesson to be taught the workers in our institutions is the lesson of *dependence upon God.* Before they can attain success in *any* line, they must, each for himself, accept the truth contained in the words of Christ: 'Without me ye can

do nothing.' "[2] Christianity—and thus Seventh-day Adventism—is about being with Jesus. Prayer is the primary medium for this to occur.

So are you a person who prays occasionally? Or are you a person *of* prayer? Joy in Christ—and if I can be so bold, revitalization in the Adventist school system—depends on one's answer to this question.

2. *Live the Word of God.* "Let nothing, however dear, however loved, absorb your mind and affections, diverting you from the study of God's Word or from earnest prayer."[3] Prayer should never take place in a vacuum, but rather is to be informed and guided by the Word of God. But the Word is to direct not only our prayers but our entire lives. Is there any part of your life that's out of step with the Bible? Confess it and ask God for strength to change. Does some impurity that the Bible condemns lurk in your life? Share it with Jesus and receive His victory over it. Is there a neighbor or coworker that Christ has been prodding you to share your faith with, but you've resisted? Confess it, ask for strength, and share life in Jesus with that person.

If this sounds simple, it is. We have made Christianity difficult, in large part because we no longer read the Bible very much. And as a consequence, life in our schools has become hard at times as well. But the simplest Christian living out the words of the Bible by Christ's power will excel in true living far beyond even the most intelligent person who ignores the Word. Revival depends upon our willingness to surrender all to Jesus—that is, to willingly fall into line with the joy-generating commands of the Bible.

3. *Receive the filling of the Holy Spirit daily.* If you think that this step is "too spiritual" and thus out of place in a book on reviving Adventist education, you have sorely underestimated the power of evil—and the power of God. The Holy Spirit is the presence of Jesus on earth. Again, Jesus Himself pointed out that "if a man remains in me and I in him, he will bear much fruit; apart from me you can do nothing" (John 15:5). Since the presence of Christ in our lives depends upon the indwelling of the Holy Spirit, one would think that we would hear much more than we do about being filled with the Spirit. Yet we don't . . . and perhaps it explains much of the dryness of our spiritual experience today, both in and out of our schools!

"But why be concerned about being filled with the Spirit?" some might say. "After all, don't we automatically receive the Holy Spirit just by being Christians?" The answer is yes . . . but no. It's true that we receive the Holy

Spirit—a measure of it—at baptism. But we are not to merely receive a measure of it—we are to be *filled* with the Spirit every day (Luke 1:15, 41, 67; 2:40; Acts 2:4; 4:8, 31; 9:17; 13:9; Eph. 5:18)! On a daily basis we are to live filled to the maximum with the Spirit of God so that we might better know Christ's will and have the strength and courage to do it.

And how do we receive the Holy Spirit? Jesus in Luke 11:11-13 makes it clear:

"Which of you fathers, if your son asks for a fish, will give him a snake instead? Or if he asks for an egg, will give him a scorpion? If you then, though you are evil, know how to give good gifts to your children, how much more will your Father in heaven give the Holy Spirit *to those who ask him!*"

If we wish to be filled with the Holy Spirit, we must request it! Why? Because it forces us to acknowledge our great need of Jesus. We humans ask for that which we think we must have. And we ignore that which we think we do not need. To ask in prayer for the Holy Spirit to possess us is to remind us that we are not self-sufficient, and that we have a loving Savior who has provided all that we need on a daily basis.

## You Mean That's It?

These three steps, when consistently lived out in one's life, inevitably result in revival. Sure, there's more we could toss into the mix that can help things along, such as fellowship, the various spiritual disciplines, etc. But the truth is that when we become people of prayer, who by Christ's power live out the Word of God and who are filled daily with His Spirit, revival cannot help occurring. And no wonder! *For revival is just another name for "normal Christianity."*

Think carefully: Which of the three steps above is something beyond what normal Christian living is to be? Or take a lesson from the life of Lazarus. After Christ raised him from the dead—that is, after he was "revived"—did he then assume an exalted existence far beyond the mere mortals of his day, performing miracles, holding court with monarchs, floating 12 inches off the ground as he walked? No! Instead, he resumed living normally. In the same way, revival is just that—being revived, being made alive again, being restored to normal Christian living in which people live in harmony with Christ and His will and find their joy in sacrifice and service for Him.

So let me make this abundantly clear. We must at all costs become adept at the more "mechanical" skills necessary to turn a school around: fund-raising, curriculum formation, staff development, physical plant improvement, and so forth. We simply *must* hone these skills, or else we will fail. And, at the same time, in the same vein, for Christ's sake and His glory, *let us become spiritually normal!* Let us become normal Christians whom the Lord uses under the guidance of His Spirit to be incredibly effective education soldiers for Him. Allow revival to come. Choose to receive it. Permit God's will be done, in us personally and in our schools corporately. And if we do, some day soon, when Jesus returns and we rise to meet Him, we will be able to look back and say with great satisfaction, "We have fought the good fight! We have finished the race! We have kept the faith! Now there is in store for us the crown of righteousness, which the Lord, the righteous Judge, is awarding us on this day—and not only to us, but also to every student who has come to long for His appearing through the ministry of our schools" (see 2 Tim. 4:7, 8).

Adventist education doesn't get any better than that!

---

[1] Ellen G. White, *Selected Messages* (Washington, D.C.: Review and Herald Pub. Assn., 1958), book 1, p. 121. (Italics supplied.)

[2] Ellen G. White, *Testimonies for the Church* (Mountain View, Calif.: Pacific Press Pub. Assn., 1948), vol. 7, p. 194. (Italics supplied.)

[3] *Ibid.,* vol. 8, p. 53.